AF553792

ACHIEVEMENT IN ENGLISH

ACHIEVEMENT IN ENGLISH

Dr. Digumarti Bhaskara Rao
Ms. Digumarti Pushpa Latha
R.V.R. College of Education
Guntur, Andhra Pradesh
(India)

DISCOVERY PUBLISHING HOUSE
NEW DELHI—110 002 (INDIA)

First Published - 1995

Reprinted - 2017

ISBN: 978-81-7141-283-9

Achievement in English

Published by:

DISCOVERY PUBLISHING HOUSE PVT. LTD.

4383/4B, Ansari Road, Darya Ganj

New Delhi-110 002 (India)

Phone: +91-11-23279245, 43596064-65

Fax: +91-11-23253475

E-mail: discoverypublishinghouse@gmail.com

sales@discoverypublishinggroup.com

web: www.discoverypublishinggroup.com

Printed at:

Infinity Imaging Systems

Delhi

FOREWORD

English has greatly contributed to the growth of knowledge in India, particularly in the fields of various sciences and in the enrichment of Indian literature. It has brought home the different developments in the international scene and helped Indians in properly understanding the world situations. Because of the great popularity and world-wide distribution, English has the pre-eminent claim to be the medium of international communication. The people around the globe are becoming closer and closer with the tremendous advancements in modern transport and communication systems. We need to have a common medium of communication to share our ideas in these close circles-English came to our help under these circumstances.

Teaching of English in Indian schools, until recently, was in a miserable state. The most unfortunate fact was the lack of any attainable aim of teaching, particularly in case of English. This aimlessness was primarily responsible for the alarming standard of achievement in English. The other limitations that arose out of and aggravated the situation were sub-standard text books, unsatisfactory evaluation systems, negative attitudes of students towards English, and dearth of competent English teachers. But in these years, due to the strenuous efforts of CIEFL and NCERT the English instruction has improved to a recognisable status, the latest models of instruction have find a place in the text books, and the evaluation process has absorbed the modern innovative language evaluation techniques.

The researchers have made a wise attempt to measure the achievement status of our secondary school students. The results of this study are not satisfactory which deserve an immediate attention. This work will serve as a model to many investigators to fill in the gap in achievement measurement in many subjects at many levels of education.

C.V.K. Narasimha Rao, B.E.
Secretary & Correspondent
S.V. College of Education
SPACES Degree College
Sri Prakash Residential Junior College
Sri Prakash Residential Model High School
Sri Prakash Vidya Niketan High School
Sri Prakash Nursery School
TUNI - 533401
East Godavari District
Andhra Pradesh
India

PREFACE

English has become an important medium of communication throughout the world. It is enjoying the status of an associate language in the official business of our government and it is there in instruction as either a second or a third language at school level. Every Indian who attends formal schooling learns English as one of the compulsory languages.

Recognising the importance of English in Indian atmosphere, a study has been undertaken to find out the achievement level at secondary school level. A reasonably large number of is taken from urban and rural, private and government, residential and non-residential, and English and Telugu-regional language - media secondary schools. Equal weightage is also given to either sex to determine achievement level in English.

The achievement of secondary school pupils in English was low. The pupils of urban, private, English medium schools and boys secured an average achievement, and only the pupils of residential schools got a high achievement. The counterparts of the above groups secured only low achievement. This result is really shocking and it raises a straight question - what went wrong with our instruction?

The teachers and pupils must work hand in hand to show their ability. The language teachers must utilise all the latest English language techniques besides mastering the content. The pupils should also attend English learning with great confidence. As language and literature make a man perfect in all walks of life, these must be mastered by the learners English.

Dr. D. Bhaskara Rao
Ms. D. Pushpa Latha

ACKNOWLEDGEMENTS

We are thankful to

Prof Talwi Marja, Estonia
Prof. Kiyoshi Amano, Japan
Prof. Miguel A. Pereyra, Granada
Prof. Marlow Ediger, U.S.A.
Prog. Skip Hills, Canada
Prof. Evelin Witruk, Germany
Prof. Ulo Vooglaid, M.P., Estonia
Prof. Ake Bjerstedt, Sweden
Dr. Teame Mebrahtu, U.K.
Dr. Kamwaruddin bin Yakub, Malaysia
Dr. Nikolina Sretenova, Bulgaria
Dr. Larissa Jogi, Estonia
Dr. Danuta Elsener, Poland
Dr. Antonin Malach, Czech
Dr. Martin McLean, U.K.
Dr. Ilze Ivanova, Latvia
Dr. Sture Norlin, Sweden
Dr. K.R.S. Sambasiva Rao, India
Dr. L. Rathaiah, India
Dr. K. Sadasiva Rao, India
Mr. C.V.K. Narasimha Rao, India
Ms. Lilian Pebre, Estonia

for their academic cooperation.

Bhaskara Rao
Pushpa Latha

CONTENTS

INTRODUCTION

Language is an interesting and exciting medium of communication. Teaching a language is still a challenging occupation. Since the nature of language and its complex operations are yet much to learn—the native language as well as a second or third language—the language teachers have an open field. They are free to experiment and innovate; they can appropriate what has proved successful in other times and other places; they can repeat and refine what they have found to be effective their own circumstances with their own students; and they can share successes and explore failures with their colleagues, learning much from each other.

Learning to use a language freely and fully is a length and effortful process. Language teachers cannot learn the language for their students. They can set their students on the road, helping them to develop confidence in their own learning powers. Then they must wait on the sidelines, ready to encourage and assist, while each student struggles and perseveres with autonomous activity. Some students learn the language well, even while the teachers observes. For those who find the task more difficult, the language teachers should atleast make every effort to ensure that their language-learning is enjoyable and educational experience. Students interested in language and uninhibited in using whatever they have assimilated will have a foundation on which to build when further opportunity presents itself. Surely all true education is beginnings.

English is one such a language followed by many people to communicate properly with each other, which needs much attention than any other language in the world. English teaching must begin with an identification of learners and an analysis of their needs. It is also necessary to answer questions which are often asked by even the educated public—why teach English as an additional language in non-English speaking nations and whether it should be taught to one and all in the schools, colleges and universities.

The question of English teaching in India is strongly linked with the status and role of English in India, and this aspect has been hitherto examined by many agencies, both private and public, but their findings seem to state not what 'is' but what 'ought to be ' the status and role of English (Sood, 1988) in free India.

The teaching of English in India dates back to the early nineteenth century. It was initially associated with the evangelical zeal of the missionaries. Later, the East India Company furthered this process in association with the British Government by trying to maintain schools for Indians. The Charter Act of 1813 signified the beginning of the East India Company's responsibility for educating Indians. It was at this time that the question of the medium of instruction raised intense controversies, but a few enlightened Indians like Raja Ram Mohan Roy felt that the system of classical education would keep the country in darkness and associated with English will be a promise of modernisation and liberation. This was the beginning of a first ever conscious attempt at English language teaching in India, but unfortunately the English teaching did not raise to the expected level though English did play a vital role in the freedom struggle and enabled the leaders to be heard abroad.

Macaualy's Minute of 1835 supported the use of English in teaching to the possible extend besides enriching the vernacular dialects. Mecaulay's Minute as accepted by Lord Bentick though protests from the vernacularists and the orientalists lingered on for a few years and this issue was settled by Lord Auckland's Minute of 1839 in favour of English conceding the need to maintain existing facilities for oriental and vernacular instruction. English and Indian languages, in the meantime, had already replaced classical languages both in education and administration by 1837. With the introduction of diarchy at the provincial level in 1921, education passed on into the hands of the elected representatives of the people which was taught in vernacular media. But, the vernacular-educated natives occupied only the lower positions both in education and administration.

When India became free on August 15, 1947 the language problem was acute. India being a multi-linguistic land, where there were 845 dialects and 15 major regional languages according to 1951 Census of India. In this linguistic situation the post-independence attempt at finding a lingua franca became a controversial issue on which no consensus could be reached. The Constitution of India, in 1950, laid down that Hindi in Devanagari script would be the official language for a period of 15 years for effecting the change over from English to Hindi. This did not settle the language controversy, but kept raging from time to time. In order to settle this controversy, the Central Advisory Board of Education, in 1956, devised a Three-Language Formula and was as accepted, in 1961, by the Conference of Chief Ministers provided for the teaching of (i) the regional language and mother tongue when the latter is different from the regional language, (ii) Hindi, or, in Hindi-speaking areas, another Indian language and (iii) English or any other modern European language.

It had become by 1959 apparent that the proposed change over from English to Hindi by 1965 was not possible and hence in 1959 Prime Minister Jawaharlal Nehru assured the non Hindi speaking people that English would continue as an associate language so long as the non-Hindi speakers wanted it, an assurance that was made under the Official Languages Act. Nehru's death, in 1964, rekindled the apprehension of non-Hindi speaking people because of the model 'may' in the text of Official Languages Act, 1963. After a great number of agitations and violence the official languages Act was amended in 1967, which provided for use of English as an Associate language without any time limit.

The restoration of English to its pre-independence status also reflected in the Three-Language Formula as modified by the Kothari Education Commission of 1964-66. Three -Language Formula as envisaged in the Commission is as mentioned herewith.

Lower Primary Stage
(classes 1 to 6—ages 6+ to 9+)

(a) Mother tongue or regional language

Higher Primary Stage
(classes 5 to 8—ages 10+ 12+)

(a) Mother tongue or regional language
(b) Hindi or English

Lower Secondary Stage
(classes 8 to 10—ages 13+ to 16+)

(a) Non-Hindi speaking areas
  (i) Mother tongue or regional language
  (ii) Hindi at higher or lower level
  (iii) English at higher or lower level
(b) Hindi speaking areas
  (i) Mother tongue or regional language
  (ii) English (or Hindi, if English has already been taken as mother tongue)
  (iii) A modern Indian language other than Hindi

Senior Secondary Stage
(classes 11 to 12—ages 17+ to 18+)

The Three-Language Formula excludes the senior secondary stage from the preview of this formula.

The revised Formula gives equal importance to both Hindi and English.

The main purpose of English teaching-learning in non-English-speaking nations is no longer literature but language, and no longer beauty and appreciation of literature but utility and practical expertise in English. Many educationists have realized that many students of English literature and language are unable to digest Shakespeare, Milton and Johnson. Still, for this present study, it is worthwhile to give an introduction of English literature to the readers to create an interest in English for further learning.

ENGLISH LITERATURE

English literature exhibits the creativity of various authors. A good sense of language helps the reader to enjoy the literature.

The Renaissance

There are times in every man's experience when some sudden widening of the boundaries of his knowledge, some vision of hitherto untried and unrealized possibilities, has come and seemed to bring with it new life and the inspiration of fresh and splendid endeavour. It may be some great book read for the first time not as a book, but as a revelation; it may be the first realization of the extent and moment of what physical science has to teach us ; it may be, like Carlyle's "Everlasting Yea," an ethical illumination, or spiritual like Augustine's or John Wesley's. But whatever it is, it brings with it new eyes, new powers of comprehension, and seems to reveal a treasury of latent and unsuspected talents in the mind and heart. The history of mankind has its parallels to these moments of illumination in the life of the individual. There are times when the boundaries of human experience, always narrow, and fluctuating but little between age and age, suddenly widen themselves, and the spirit of man leaps forward to possess and explore its new domain. These are the great ages of the world. They could be counted, perhaps, on one hand. The age of Pericles in Athens; the less defined age, when Europe passed, spiritually and artistically, from what we call the Dark, to what we call the Middle ages; the Renaissance; the period of the French Revolution. Two of them, so far as English literature is concerned, fall within the compass of this review, and it is with one of them—the Renaissance—that it begins.

It is as difficult to find a comprehensive formula for what the Renaissance meant as to tie it down to a date. The year 1453 A.D., when the Eastern Empire — the last relic of the continuous spirit of Rome -- fell before the Turks, used to be given as the date, and perhaps the word "Renaissance" itself—"a new birth"— is as much as can be accomplished shortly by way of definition. Michelet's resonant "discovery by mankind of himself and of the world" rather express what a man of the Renaissance himself must have thought it, than what we in this age can declare it to be. But both endeavours to date and to define are alike impossible. One cannot fix a term to day of night, and the theory of the Renaissance as a kind of tropical dawn—a sudden passage to light from darkness—is not to be considered. The Renaissance was, and was the result of, a numerous and various series of events which followed and accompanied one another from the fourteenth to the beginning of the sixteenth centuries, First and most immediate in its influence on art and literature and thought, was the rediscovery of the ancient literatures. In the Middle ages knowledge of Greek and Latin literatures had withdrawn itself into monasteries, and there narrowed till of secular Latin writing scarcely any knowledge remained save of Vergil (because of his supposed Messianic prophecy) and Statius, and of Greek, except Aristotle, none at all. What had been lost in the Western Empire, however, subsisted in the East, and the continual advance of the Turk on the territories of the Emperors of Constantinople drove westward to the shelter of Italy and the Church and to the patronage of the Medicis, a crowd of scholars who brought with them their manuscripts of Homer and the dramatists, of Thucydides and Herodotus, and most momentous perhaps for the age to come, of Plato and Demosthenes and of the New Testament in its original Greek. The quick and vivid intellect of Italy, which had been torpid in the decadence of mediaevalism and its mysticism and piety, seized with avidity the revelation of the classical world which the scholars and their manuscripts brought. Human life, which the mediaeval Church had taught them to regard but as a threshold and stepping-stone to eternity, acquired suddenly a new momentousness and value; the promises of the Church paled like its lamps at sunrise; and a new paganism, which had Plato for its high priest, and Demosthenes and Pericles for its archetypes and examples, ran like wild-fire through Italy. The Greek spirit seized on art, and produced Raphael, Leonardo, and Michel Angelo; on literature and philosophy and gave us the Pico della Mirrandula, on life and gave us the Medicis and Castiglione and Machiavelli. Then—the invention not of Italy but of Germany—came the art of printing, and made this revival of Greek literature quickly portable into other lands.

Even more momentous was the new knowledge the age brought of the physical world. The brilliant conjectures of Copernicus paved the way for Galileo, and the warped and narrow cosmology which conceived the earth as the centre of the universe, suffered a blow that in shaking it shook also religion. And while the conjectures of the men of science were adding regions undreamt of to the physical universe, the discoverers were enlarging the territories of the earth itself. The Portuguese, with the aid of sailors trained in the great Mediterranean ports of Genoa and Venice, pushed the track of exploration down the western coast of Africa: the Cape was circumnavigated by Vasco da Gama, and India reached for the first time by Western men by way of the sea. Columbus reached Trinidad and discovered the "New " World: his successors pushed past him and touched the Continent. Spanish colonies grew up along the coasts of North and Central America and in Peru, and the Portuguese reached Brazil. Cabot and the English voyagers reached Newfoundland and Labrador; the French made their way up the St. Lawrence. The discovery of the gold mines brought new and unimagined possibilities of wealth to the Old World, while the imagination of Europe, bounded since the beginning of recorded time by the Western ocean, and with the Mediterranean as its center, shot out to the romance and mystery of untried seas.

It is difficult for us in these later days to conceive the profound and stirring influence of such an alteration on thought and literature. To the men at the end of the fifteenth century scarcely a year but brought another bit of received and recognized thinking to the scrap heap; scarcely a year but some new discovery found itself surpassed and in its turn discarded, or lessened in significance by something still more new. Columbus sailed westward to find a new sea route, and as he imagined, a more expeditious one to "the Indies"; the name West Indies still survives to show the theory on which the early discoverers worked. The rapidity with which knowledge widened can be gathered by a comparison of the maps of the day. In the earlier of them the mythical Brazil, a relic perhaps of the lost Atlantis, lay a regularly and mystically blue island off the west coast of Ireland; then the Azores were discovered and the name fastened on to one of the islands of that archipelago. Then Amerigo reached South America and the name became finally fixed to the country that we know. There is nothing nowadays that can give us a parallel to the stirring and exaltation of the imagination which intoxicated the men of the Renaissance, and gave a new birth to thought and art. The great scientific discoveries of the nineteenth century came to men more prepared for the shock of new surprises, and they carried evidence less tangible and indisputable to the senses. Perhaps if the strivings of science should succeed in proving as evident and comprehensible the existences which spiritualist and psychical research is striving to establish, we should know the thrill that the great twin discoverers, Copernicus and Columbus, brought to Europe.

This rough sketch of the Renaissance has been set down because it is only by realizing the period in its largest and broadest sense, that we can understand the beginnings of our own modern literature. The renaissance reached England late. By the time that the impulse was at its height with Spenser and Shakespeare, it had died out in Italy, and in France to which in its turn Italy had passed the torch, it was already a waning fire. When it came to England it came in a special form shaped by political and social conditions, and by the accidents of temperament and inclination in the men who began the movement. But the essence of the inspiration remained the same as it had been on the Continent, and the twin threads of its two main impulses, the impulse from the study of the classics, and the impulse given to men's minds by the voyages of discovery, runs through all the texture of our Renaissance literature.

Literature as it developed in the reign of Elizabeth ran counter to the hopes and desires of the men who began the movement; the common usage which extends the term Elizabethan backwards outside the limits of the reign itself, has nothing but its carelessness to recommend it. The men of the early renaissance in the reigns of Edward VI and Mary, belonged to a graver school than their successors. They were no splendid courtiers, nor daring and hardy adventurers, still less swashbucklers, exquisites, or literary dandies. Their names — Sir John Cheke, Roger Ascham, Nicholas Udall, Thomas Wilson, Walter Haddon, belong rather to the universities and to the coteries of learning, than to the court. To the nobility, from whose essays and *belles letters* Elizabethan poetry was to develop, they stood in the relation of tutors rather than of companions, suspecting the extravagances of their pupils rather than sympathizing with their ideals. They were a band of serious and dignified scholars, men preoccupied with morality and good-citizenship, and holding those as worth more than the lighter interests of learning and style. It is perhaps characteristic of the English temper that the revival of the lassical tongues, which in Italy made for paganism, and the pursuit of pleasure in life and art, in England brought with it in the first place a new seriousness and gravity of life, and in religion the Reformation. But in a way the scholars fought against tendencies in their age, which were both too fast and too strong for them. At a time when young men were writing poetry modelled on the delicate and extravagant verse of Italy, were reading Italian novels, and affecting Italian fashions in speech and dress, they were fighting for sound education, for good classical scholarship, for the purity of native English, and behind all these for the native strength and worth of the English character, which they felt to be endangered by orgies or reckless assimilation from abroad. The revival of the classics at Oxford and Cambridge could not produce an Erasmus or a Scaliger; we have no fine critical scholarship of this age to put beside that of Holland or France. Sir John Cheke and his followers felt they had a public and national duty to perform, and their knowledge of the classics only served them for examples of high living and morality, on which education, in its sense of the formation of character, could be based.

The literary influence of the revival of letters in England, apart from its moral influence, took two contradictory and opposing forms. In the curricula of schools, logic, which in the Middle Ages had been the groundwork of thought and letters, gave place to rhetoric. The reading of the ancients awakened new delight in the melody and beauty of language: men became intoxicated with words. The practice of rhetoric was universal and it quickly coloured all literature. It was the habit of the rhetoricians to chose some subject for declamation and round it to encourage their pupils to set embellishments and decorations, which commonly proceeded rather from a delight in language for language's sake, than from any effect in enforcing an argument. Their models for these exercises can be traced in their influence on later writers. One of the most popular of them, Erasmus's "Discourse Persuading a Young Man to Marriage," which was translated in an English Text-book of rhetoric, reminds one of the first part of Shakespeare's sonnets. The literary affectation called euphuism was directly based on the precepts of the handbooks on rhetoric; its author, John Lyly, only elaborated and made more Precise tricks of phrase and writing, which had been used as exercises in the schools of his youth. The prose of his school, with its fantastic delight in exuberance of figure and sound, owed its inspiration, in its form ultimately to Cicero, and in the decorations with which it was embellished, to the elder Pliny and later writers of his kind. The long declamatory speeches and the sententiousness of the early drama were directly modelled on Seneca, through whom was faintly reflected the tragedy of Greece, unknown directly or almost unknown to English readers. Latinism, like every new craze, became a passion, and ran through the less intelligent kinds of writing in a wild excess. Not much of the literature of this time remains in common·knowledge, and for examples of these affectations one must turn over the black letter pages of forgotten books. There high-sounding and familiar words are handled and bandied about with delight, and you can see in volume after volume these minor and forgotten authors gloating over the new found treasure which placed them in their time in the van of literary success. That they are obsolete now, and indeed were obsolete before they were dead, is a warning to authors who intend similar extravagances. Strangeness and exoticism are not lasting wares. By the time of "Love's Labour Lost" they had become nothing more than matter of laughter, and it is only through their reflection and distortion in Shakespeare's pages that we known them now.

Had not a restraining influence, anxiously and even acrimoniously urged, broken in on their endeavours the English language to-day might have been almost as completely latinized as Spanish or Italian. That the essential Saxon purity of our tongue has been preserved is to the credit not of sensible unlettered people eschewing new fashions they could not comprehend, but to the scholars themselves. The chief service that Cheke and Ascham and their fellows rendered to English literature was their crusade against the exaggerated latinity that they had themselves helped to make possible, the crusade against what they called "inkhorn terms." "I am of this opinion," said Cheke in a prefatory letter to a book translated by a friend of his, "that our own tongue should be written clean and pure, unmixed and unmangled with the borrowing of other tongues, wherein if we take not heed by time, ever borrowing and never paying, she shall be fain to keep her house as bankrupt." Writings in the Saxon vernacular like the sermons of Latimer, who was careful to use nothing not familiar to the common people, did much to help the scholars to save our prose from the extravagances which they dreaded. Their attack was directed no less against the revival of really obsolete words. It is a paradox worth noting for its strangeness that the first revival of mediaevalism in modern English literature was in the Renaissance itself. Talking in studious archaism seems to have been a fashionable practice in society and court circles. "The fine courtier," says Thomas Wilson in his *Art of Rhetoric*, "will talk nothing but Chaucer." The scholars of the English Renaissance fought not only against the ignorant adoption of their importations, but against the renewal of forgotten habits of speech.

Their efforts failed, and their ideals had to wait for their acceptance till the age of Dryden, when Shakespeare and Spenser and Milton, all of them authors who consistently violated the standards of Cheke, had done their work. The fine courtier who would talk nothing but Chaucer was in Elizabeth's reign the saving of English verse. The beauty and richness of spenser is based directly on words he got from *Troilus* and *Cressida* and the *Canterbury Tales*. Some of the most sonorous and beautiful lines in Shakespeare break every cannon laid down by the humanists.

"The' extravagant and erring spirit hies
To his confine"

is a line, three of the chief words of which are Latin importations that come unfamiliarly, bearing their original interpretation with them. Milton is packed with similar things: he will talk of a crowded meeting as "frequent" and use constructions which are unintelligible to anyone who does not possess a knowledge—and a good knowledge—of Latin syntax. Yet the effect is a good poetic effect. In attacking latinisms in the language borrowed from older poets Cheke and his companions were attacking the two chief sources of Elizabethan poetic vocabulary. All the sonorousness, beauty and dignity of the poetry and the drama which followed them would have been lost had they succeeded in their object , and their verse would have been constrained into the warped and ugly forms of Sternhold and Hopkins, and those with them who composed the first and worst metrical version of the Psalms. When their idea reappeared for its fulfillment phantasy and imagery had temporarily worn themselves out, and the richer language made simplicity possible and adequate for poetry.

There are other directions in which the classical revival influenced writing that need not detain us here. The attempt to transplant classical meters into English verse which was the concern of a little group of authors who called themselves the Areopagus came to no more success than a similar and contemporary attempt did in France. An earlier and more lasting result of the influence of the classics on new ways of thinking is the *Utopia* of Sir Thomas More, based on Plato's *Republic*, and followed by similar attempts on the part of other authors, of which the most notable are Harrington's *Oceana* and Bacon's *New Atlantis*. In one way or another the rediscovery of Plato proved the most valuable part of the Renaissance's gift from Greece. The doctrines of he Symposium coloured in Italy the writings of Castiglione and Mirandula. In England they gave us Spenser's "Hymn to Intellectual Beauty," and they affected, each in his own way, Sir Philip Sidney, and others of the circle of court writers of his time. More's book was written in Latin though there is an English translation almost contemporary. He combines in himself the two strains that we found working in the Renaissance, for besides its origin in Plato, Utopia owes not a little to the influence of the voyages of discovery. In 1507 there was published a little book called an *Introduction to Cosmography*, which gave an account of the four voyages of Amerigo. In the story of the fourth voyage it is narrated that twenty-four men were left in a fort near Cape Bahia. More used this detail as a starting-point, and one of the men whom Amerigo left tells the story of this "Nowhere," a republic partly resembling England but most of all the ideal, world of Plato. Partly resembling England, because no man can escape from the influences of his own time, whatever road he takes, whether the road of imagination or any other. His imagination can only build out of the materials afforded him by his own experience; he can alter, he can rearrange, but he cannot in the strictest sense of the word create, and every city of dreams is only the scheme of things as they are remoulded nearer to the desire of a man's heart. In a way More has less invention than some of his subtler followers, but his book is interesting because it is the first example of a kind of writing which has been attractive to many men since his time, and particularly to writers of our own day.

There remains one circumstance in the revival of the classes which had a marked and continuous influence on the literary age that followed. To get the classics English scholars had as we have seen to go to Italy. Cheke went there and so did Wilson, and the path of travel across France and through Lombardy to Florence and Rome was worn hard by the feet of their followers for over a hundred years after. On the heels of the men of learning went the men of fashion, eager to lean and copy the new manners of a society whose moral teacher was Machiavelli, and whose patterns of splendour were the courts of Florence and Ferrara, and to learn the trick of verse that in the hands of Petrarch and his followers had fashioned the sonnet and other new lyric forms. This could not be without its influence on the manners of the nation, and the scholars who had been the first to show the way were the first to deplore the pell-mell assimilation of Italian manners and vices, which was the unintended result of the inroad on insularity which had already begun. They saw the danger ahead, and they laboured to meet it as it came. Ascham in his *Schoolmaster* railed against the translation of Italian books, and the corrupt manners of living and false ideas which they seemed to him to breed. The Italianate Englishman became the chief part of the stock-in-trade of the satirists and moralists of the day. Stubbs, a Puritan chronicler, whose book. *The Anatomy of Abuses* is a valuable aid to the study of Tudor social history, and Harrison, whose description of England preface Holinshed's Chronicles, both deal in detail with the Italian menace, and condemn in good set terms the costliness in dress and the looseness in morals which they laid to its charge. Indeed, the effect on England was profound, and it lasted for more than two generations. The romantic traveller, Coryat, writing well within the seventeenth century in praise of the luxuries of Italy (among which he numbers forks for table use), is as enthusiastic as the authors who began the imitation of Italian meters in Tottel's *Miscellany*, and Donne and Hall in their satires written under James wield the rod of censure as sternly as had Ascham a good half century before. No doubt there was something in the danger they dreaded, but the evil was not unmixed with good, for insularity will always be an enemy of good literature. The Elizabethans learned much more than their plots from Italian models, and the worst effects dreaded by the patriots neve reached our shores. Italian vice stopped short of real life; poisoning and hired ruffianism flourished only on the stage.

The influence of the spirit of discovery and adventure, though it is less quickly marked, more pervasive, and less easy to define, is perhaps more universal than that of the classics or of the Italian fashions which came in their train. It runs right through the literature of Elizabeth's age and after it, affecting, each in their special way, all the dramatists, authors who were also adventures like Raleigh, scholars like Milton, and philosophers like Hobbes and Locke. It reappears in the Romantic revival with Coleridge, whose "Ancient Mariner" owes much to reminiscences of his favourite reading—*Purchas, his Pilgrimes*, and other old books of voyages. The matter of this too-little noticed strain in English literature would suffice to fill a whole book; only a few of the main lines of its influence can be noted here.

For the English Renaissance—for Elizabeth's England, action and imagination went hand in hand; the dramatists and poets held up the mirror to the voyagers. In a sense, the cult of the sea is the oldest note in English literature. There is not a poem in Anglo-Saxon but breathes the saltness and the bitterness of the sea-air. To the old English the sea was something inexpressibly melancholy and desolate, mist-shrouded, and lonely, terrible in its grey and shivering spaces; and their tone about it is always elegiac and plaintive, as a place of dreary spiritless wandering and unmarked graves. When the English settled they lost the sense of the sea; they became a little parochial people, tilling fields and tending cattle, wool-gathering and wool, bartering, their shipping confined to cross-Channel merchandise, and coastwise sailing from port to port. Chaucer's shipman, almost the sole representative of the sea in medieval English literature, plied a coastwise trade. But with the Cabots and their followers, Frobisher and Gilbert and Drake and Hawkins, all this was changed; once more the ocean became the highway of our national progress and adventure, and by virtue of our shipping we became competitors for the dominion of the earth. The rising tide of national enthusiasm and exaltation that this occasioned flooded popular literature. The voyagers themselves wrote down the stories of their adventures; and collections of these—Hakluyt's and Purcha's—were among the most popular books of the age. To them, indeed, we must look for the first beginnings of our modern English prose, and some of its noblest passages. The writers, as often as not, were otherwise utterly unknown—ship's pursers, supper-cargoes, and the like—men without much literary craft or training, whose style is great because of the greatness of their subject, because they had no literary artifices to stand between them and the plain and direct telling of a stirring tale. But the ferment worked outside the actual doings of the voyagers themselves, and it can be traced beyond definite allusions to them. Allusions, indeed, are surprisingly few; Drake is scarcely as much as mentioned among the greater writers of the age. None the less there is not one of them that is not deeply touched by his spirit and that of the movement which he led. New lands had been discovered, new territories opened up, wonders exposed which were perhaps only the first fruits of greater wonders to come. Spenser makes the voyagers his warrant for his excursion into fairyland. Some, he says, have condemned his fairy world as an idle fiction.

> "But let that man with better advice;
> That of the world least part to us is red;
> And daily how through hardy enterprise
> Many great regions are discovered,
> Which to late age were never mentioned.
> Who ever heard of the 'Indian Peru'?
> Or who in venturous vessel measured
> The Amazon, huge river, now found true?
> Or fruitfullest Virginia who did ever view?
>
> Yet all these were when no man did them know,
> Yet have from wiser ages hidden been;
> And later times things more unknown shall
> show."

It is in the drama that this spirit of adventure caught from the voyagers gets its full play. "Without the voyagers," says Professor Walter Raleigh, "Marlowe is inconceivable." His imagination in every one of his plays is preoccupied with the lust of adventure, and the wealth and power adventure brings. Tamburlaine, Eastern conqueror though he is, is at heart and Englishman of the school of Hawkins and Drake. Indeed the comparison must have occurred to his own age, for a historian of the day, the antiquary Stow, declares Drake to have been "as famous in Europe and America as Tamburlaine was in Asia and Africa." The high-sounding names and quests which seem to us to give the play an air of unreality and romance were to the Elizabethans real and actual; things as strange and foreign were to be heard any day amongst the motley crowd in the Bankside outside the theatre door. Tamburlaine's last speech when he calls for a map and points the way to unrealized conquests, is the very epitome of the age of discovery.

"Lo, here my sons, are all the golden mines,
Inestimable wares and precious stones,
More worth than Asia and all the world beside;
And from the Antarctic Pole eastward behold
As much more land, which never was descried,
Wherein are rocks of pearl that shine as bright
As all the lamps that beautify the sky."

It is the same in his other plays. Dr. Faustus assigns to his serviceable spirits tasks that might have been studied from the books of Hakluyt.

"I'll have them fly to India for gold,
Ransack the ocean for orient pearl,
And search all corners of the new round world
For pleasant fruits and princely delicates."

When there is no actual expression of the spirit of adventure, the air of the sea which it carried with it still blows. Shakespeare, save for his scenes in *The Tempest* and in *Pericles*, which seize in all its dramatic poignancy the terror of storm and shipwreck, has nothing dealing directly with the sea or with travel, but it comes out, none the less, in figure and metaphor, an plays like the *Merchant of Venice* and *Othello* testify to his accessibility to its spirit. Milton, a scholar whose mind was occupied by other and more ultimate matters, is full of allusions to it. Satan's journey through Chaos in *Paradise Lost* is the occasion for a whole series of metaphors drawn from seafaring. In *Samson Agonistes* Dalila comes in.

"Like a stately ship..........
With all her bravery on and tackle trim
Sails frilled and streamers waving
Courted by all the winds that hold them play.

and Samson speaks of himself as one who,

"Like a foolish pilot have shipwrecked
My vessel trusted to me from above
Gloriously rigged."

The influence of the voyages of discovery persisted long after the first bloom of the Renaissance had flowered and withered. On the reports brought home by the voyagers were founded in part those conceptions of the condition of the "natural" man which form such a large part of the philosophic discussions of the seventeenth and eighteenth centuries. Hobbes's description of the life of nature as "nasty, solitary, brutish, and short," Locke's theories of civil government, and eighteenth century speculators like Monboddo all took as the basis of their theory the observations of the men of travel. Abroad this connection of travellers and philosophers was no less intimate. Both Montesquieu and Rousseau owed much to the tales of the Iroquois, the North American Indian allies of France. Locke himself is the best example of the closeness of this alliance. He was a diligent student of the texts of the voyagers, and himself edited out of Hakluyt and Purchas the best collection of them current in his day. The purely literary influence of the age of discovery persisted down to *Robinson Crusoe*; in that book by a refinement of satire a return to travel itself (it must be remembered Defoe posed not as a novelist but as an actual traveller) is used to make play with the deduction founded on it. Crusoe's conversation with the man Friday will be found to be a satire of Locke's famous controversy with the Bishop of Worcester. With *Robinson Crusoe* the influence of the age of discovery finally perishes. An inspiration hardens into the mere subject matter of books of adventure. We need not follow it further.

The Elizabethan Poetry

To understand Elizabethan literature it is necessary to remember that the social status it enjoyed was far different from that of literature in our own day. The splendours of the Medicis in Italy had set up an ideal of courtliness, in which letters formed an integral and indispensable part. For the Renaissance, the man of letters was only one aspect of the gentleman, and the true gentleman, as books so early and late respectively as Castiglione's *Courtier* and Peacham's *Complete Gentleman* show, numbered poetry as a necessary part of his accomplishments. In England special circumstances intensified this tendency of the time. The queen was unmarried: she was the first single woman to wear the English crown, and her vanity made her value the devotion of the men about her as something more intimate than mere loyalty or patriotism. She loved personal homage, particularly the homage of half-amatory eulogy in prose and verse. It followed that the ambition of every courtier was to be an author, and of every author to be a courtier; in fact, outside the drama, which was almost the only popular writing at the time, every author was in a greater or less degree attached to the court. If they were not enjoying its favours they were pleading for them, mingling high and fantastic compliment with bitter reproaches and a tale of misery. And consequently both the poetry and the prose of the time are restricted in their scope and temper to the artificial and romantic, to high-flown eloquence, to the celebration of love and devotion, or to the inculcation of those courtly virtues and accomplishments which composed the perfect pattern of a gentleman. Not that there was not both poetry and prose written outside this charmed circle. The pamphleteers and chroniclers, Dekker and Nash, Holinshed and Harrison and Stow, were setting down their histories and descriptions, and penning those detailed and realistic indictments of the follies and extravagances of fashion, which together with the comedies have enabled us to picture accurately the England and especially the London of Elizabeth's reign. There was fine poetry written by Marlowe and Chapman as a well as by Sidney and Spenser, but the court was still the main centre of literary endeavour, and the main incitement to literary fame and success.

But whether an author was a courtier or a Londoner living by his wits, writing was never the main business of his life: all the writers of the time were in one way or another men of action and affairs. As later as Milton it is probably true to say that writing was in the case even of the greatest an avocation, something indulged in at leisure outside a man's main business. All the Elizabethan authors had crowded and various careers. Of Sir Philip Sidney his earliest biographer says, "The truth is his end was not writing, even while he wrote, but both his wit and understanding bent upon his heart to make himself and others not in words or opinion but in life and action good and great." Ben Johnson was in turn a soldier, a poet, a bricklayer, an actor, and ultimately the first poet laureate. Lodge, after leaving Oxford, passed through the various professions of soldiering, medicine, play writing, and fiction, and he wrote his novel *Rosalind*, on which Shakespeare based *As You Like It*, while he was sailing on a piratical venture on the Spanish Main. This connection between life and action affected as we have seen the tone and quality of Elizabethan writing. "All the distinguished writers of the period," says Thoreau, "possess a greater vigour and naturalness than the more modern. . . you have constantly the warrant of life and experience in what you read. The little that is said is eked out by implication of the much that was done." In another passage the same writer explains the strength and fineness of the writings of Sir Walter Raleigh by this very test of action, "The word which is best said came nearest to not being spoken at all, for it is cousin to a deed which the speaker could have better done. Nay almost it must have taken the place of a deed by some urgent necessity, even by some misfortune, so that the truest writer will be some captive knight after all." This bond between literature and action explains more than the writings of the voyageres or the pamphlets of men who lived in London by what they could make of their fellows. Literature has always a two-fold relation to life as it is lived. It is both a mirror and an escape: in our own day the stirring romances of Stevenson, the full-blooded and vigorous life which beats through the pages of Mr. Kipling, the conscious brutalism of such writers as Conrad and Mr. Hewlett, the plays of J.M. Synge, occupied with the vigorous and coarse-grained life of tinkers and peasants, are all in their separate ways a reaction against an age in which the overwhelming majority of men and women have sedentary pursuits. Just in the same way the Elizabethan who passed his commonly short and crowded life in an atmosphere of throat-cutting and powder and shot, and in a time when affairs of state were more momentous for the future of the nation than they have ever been since, needed his escape from the things which pressed in upon his every day. So grew the vogue and popularity of pastoral poetry and the pastoral romance.

It is with two courtiers that modern English poetry begins. The lives of Sir Thomas Wyatt and the Earl of Surrey both ended early and unhappily, and it was not until ten years after the death of the second of them that their poems appeared in print. The book that contained them, Tottel's *Miscellany of Songs and Sonnets*, is one of the landmarks of English literature. It begins lyrical love poetry in our language. It begins, too, the imitation and adaptation of foreign and chiefly Italian metrieal forms, many of which have since become characteristic forms of English verse: so characteristic, that we scarcely thing of them as other than native in origin. To Wyatt belongs the honour of introducing the sonnet, and to Surrey the more momentous credit of writing, for the first time in English, blank verse. Wyatt fills the most important place in the *Miscellany*, and his work, experimental in tone and quality, formed the example which Surrey and minor writers in the same volume and ali the later poets of the age copied. He tries his hand at everything—songs, madrigals, elegies, complaints, and sonnets—and he takes his models from both ancient Rome and modern Italy. Indeed there is scarcely anything in the volume for which with some trouble and research one might not find an original in Petrarch, or in the poets of Italy who followed him. But imitation, universal though it is in his work, does not altogether crowd out originality of feeling and poetic temper. At times, be sounds a personal note, his joy on leaving Spain for England, his feeling in the Tower, his life at the Court amongst his books, and as a country gentleman enjoying hunting and other outdoor sports.

> "This maketh me at home to hunt and hawks,
> And in foul weather at my book to sit,
> In frost and snow, then with my bow to stalk,
> No man does mark whereas I ride or go:
> In lusty less at liberty I walk."

It is easy to see that poetry as a melodious and enriched expression of a man's own feelings is in its infancy here. The new poets had to find their own language, to enrich with borrowings from other tongues the stock of words suitable for poetry which the dropping of inflection had left to English. Wyatt was at the beginning of the process, and apart from a gracious and courtly temper, his work has, it must be confessed, hardly more than an antiquarian interest. Surrey, it is possible to say on reading his work, went one step further. He allows himself oftener the luxury of a reference to personal feelings, and his poetry contains from place to place a fairly full record of the vicissitudes of his life. A prisoner at Windsor, he recalls his childhood there

> "The large green courts where we were wont to hove,
> The palme-play, where, despoiled for the game,
> With dazzled eyes oft we by gleams of love
> Have missed the ball, and got sight of or dame."

Like Wyatt's, his verses are poor stuff, but a sympathetic ear can catch in them something of the accent that distinguishes the verse of Sidney and Spenser. He is greater than Wyatt, not so much for greater skill as for more boldness in experiment. Wyatt in his sonnets had used the Petrarchan or Italian form, the form used later in England by Milton and in the nineteenth century by Rossetti. He built up each poem, that is, in two parts, the octave, a two-rhymed section of eight lines at the beginning, followed by the sestet, a six line close with three rhymes. The form fits itself very well to the double mood which commonly inspires a poet using the sonnet form; the second section as it were both echoing and answering the first, following doubt with hope, or sadness with resignation, or resolving a problem set itself by the heart. Surrey tried another manner, the manner which by its use in Shakespeare's sonnets has come to be regarded as the English form of this kind of lyric. His sonnets are virtually three stanza poems with a couplet for close, and he allows himself as many rhymes as he chooses. The structure is obviously easier, and it gives a better chance to an inferior workman, but in the hands of a master its harmonies are no less delicate, and its capacity to represent changing modes of thought no less complete than those of the true form of Petrach. Blank verse, which was Surrey's other gift to English poetry, was in a way a compromise between the two sources from which the English Renaissance drew its inspiration. Latin and Greek verse is quantitative and rhymeless; Italian verse, built up on the meters of the troubadours and the degeneration of Latin which gave the world the Romance languages, used many elaborate forms of rhyme. Blank verse took from Latin its rhymelessness, but it retained accent instead of quantity as the basis of its line. The line Surrey used is the five-foot or ten-syllable line of what is called "heroic verse"—the line used by Chaucer in his Prologue and most of his tales. Like Milton he deplored rhyme as the invention of a barbarous age, and no doubt he would have rejoiced to go further and banish accent as well as rhymed endings. That, however, was not to be, though in the best blank verse of later time accent and quantity both have their share in the effect. The instrument he forged passed into the hands of the dramatists: Marlowe perfected its rhythm, Shakespeare broke its monotony and varied its cadences by altering the spacing of the accents, and occasionally be adding an extra unaccented syllable. It came back from the drama to poetry with Milton. His blindness and the necessity under which it laid him of keeping in his head long stretches of verse at one time, because he could not look back to see what he had written, probably helped his naturally quick and delicate sense of cadence to vary the pauses, so that a variety of accent and interval might replace the valuable aid to memory which he put aside in putting aside rhyme. Perhaps it is to two accidents, the accident by which blank verse as the medium of the actor had to be retained easily in the memory, and the accident of Milton's blindness, that must be laid the credit of more than a little of the richness of rhythm of this, the chief and greatest instrument of English verse.

The imitation of Italian and French forms which Wyatt and Surrey began, was continued by a host of younger amateurs of poetry. Laborious research has indeed found a Continental original for almost every great poem of the time, and for very many forgotten ones as well. It is easy for the student engaged in this kind of literary exploration to exaggerate the importance of what he finds, and of late years criticism, written mainly by these explorers, has tended to assume that since it can be found that Sidney, and Daniel, and Watson, and all the other writers of mythological poetry and sonnet sequences took their ideas and their phrases from foreign poetry, their work is therefore to be classed merely as imitative literary expertise, that it is frigid, that it contains or conveys no real feeling, and that except in the secondary and derived sense, it is not really lyrical at all. Petrarch, they will tell you, may have felt deeply and sincerely about Laura, but when Sidney uses Petrarch's imagery and even translates his words in order to express his feelings for Stella, he is only a plagiarist and not a lover, and the passion for Lady Rich which is supposed to have inspired his sonnets, nothing more than a not too seriously intended trick to add the excitement of a transcript of real emotion to what was really an academic exercise. If that were indeed so, then Elizabethan poetry is a very much lesser and meaner thing than later ages have thought it. But is it so? Let us look into the matter a little more closely. The unit of all ordinary kinds of writing is the word, and one is not commonly quarrelled with for using words that have belonged to other people. But the unit of the lyric, like the unit of spoken conversation, is not the word but the phrase. Now in daily human intercourse the use, which is universal and habitual, of set forms and phrases of talk is not commonly supposed to detract from, or destroy sincerity. In the crises indeed of emotion it must be most people's experience that the natural speech that rises unbidden and easiest to the lips is something quite familiar and commonplace, some form which the accumulated experience of many generations of separate people has found best for such circumstances or such an occasion. The lyric is just in the position of conversation, at such a heightened and emotional moment. It is the speech of deep feeling, that must be articulate or choke, and it falls naturally and inevitably into some form which accumulated passionate moments have created and fixed. The course of emotional experiences differs very little from age to age, and from individual to individual, and so the same phrases may be used quite sincerely and naturally as the direct expression of feeling at its highest point by men apart in country, circumstances, or time. This is not to say that there is so such thing as originality; a poet is a poet first and most of all because he discovers truths that have been known for ages, as things that are fresh and new and vital for himself. He must speak of them in language that has been used by other men just because they are known truths, but he will use that language in a new way, and with a new significance, and it is just in proportion to the freshness, and the air of personal conviction and sincerity which he imparts to it, that he is great.

The point at issue bears very directly on the work of Sir Philip Sidney. In the course of the history of English letters certain authors disengage themselves who have more than a merely literary position: they are symbolic of the whole age in which they live, its life and action, its thoughts and ideals, as well as its mere modes of writings. There are not many of them and they could be easily numbered; Addison, perhaps, certainly Dr. Johnson, certainly Byron, and in the later age probably Tennyson. But the greatest of them all is Sir Philip Sidney: his symbolical relation to the time in which he lived was realized by his contemporaries, and it has been a commonplace of history and criticism ever since. Elizabeth called him one of the jewels of her crown, and at the age of twenty-three, so fast did genius ripen in that summer time of the Renaissance, William the Silent could speak of him as "one of the ripest statesmen of the age." He travelled widely in Europe, knew many language, and dreamed of adventure in America and on the high seas. In a court of brilliant figures, his was the most dazzling, and his death at Zutphen only served to intensify the halo of romance which had gathered round his name. His literary exercises were various: in prose he wrote the *Arcadia* and the *Apology for Poetry*, the one the beginning of a new kind of imaginative writing, and the other the first of the series of those rare and precious commentaries on their own art which some of our English poets have left us. To the *Arcadia* we shall have to return later in this chapter. It is his other great work, the sequence of sonnets entitled *Astrophel and Stella*, which concerns us here. They celebrate the history of his love for Penelope Devereux, sister of the Earl of Essex, a love brought to disaster by the intervention of queen Elizabeth with whom he had quarreled. As poetry they mark an epoch. They are the first direct expression of an intimate and personal experience in English literature, struck off in the white heat of passion, and though they are coloured at times with that over-fantastic imagery which is at once a characteristic fault and excellence of the writing of the time, they never lose the one merit above all others of lyric poetry, the merit of sincerity. The note is struck with certainty and power in the first sonnet of the series:-

> "Loving in truth, and fain in verse my love to
> show,
> That she, dear she, might take some pleasure of
> my pain,—
> Pleasure might cause her read, reading might
> make her know,—
> Knowledge might pity win, and pity grace ob-
> tain,—
> I sought fit words to paint the blackest face of
> woe,
> Studying inventions fine her wits to entertain;
> Oft turning others' leaves to see if thence would
> flow
> Some fresh and fruitful flower upon my sun-
> burned brain.
> But words came halting forth. . .
> Biting my truant pen, beating myself for spite.
> Fool,' said my muse to me, 'look in thy heart
> and write.'"

And though he turned others' leaves it was quite literally looking in his heart that he wrote. He analyses the sequence of his feelings with a vividness and minuteness which assure us of their truth. All that he tells is the fruit of experience, dearly bought:

> "Desire ! desire ! I have too dearly bought
> With price of mangled mind thy worthless ware.
> Too long, too long! asleep thou hast me brought,
> Who shouldst my mind to higher things prepare."

and earlier in the sequence—

> "I now have learned love right and learned even so
> As those that being poisoned poison know."

In the last two sonnets, with crowning truth and pathos he renounces earthly love which reaches but to dust, and which because it fades brings but fading pleasure:

> "Then farewell, world! Thy uttermost I see.
> Eternal love, maintain thy life in me."

The sonnets were published after Sidney's death, and it is certain that like Shakespeare's they were never intended for publication at all. The point is important because it helps to vindicate Sidney's sincerity, but were nay vindication needed another more certain might be found. The *Arcadia* is strewn with love songs and sonnets, the exercises solely of the literary imagination. Let any one who wishes to gauge the sincerity of the impulse of the Stella sequence compare any of the poems in it with those in the romance.

With Sir Philip Sidney literature was an avocation, constantly indulged in, but outside the main business of his life; with Edmund Spenser public life and affairs were subservient to an overmastering poetic impulse. He did his best to carve out a career for himself like other young men of his time, followed the fortunes of the Earl of Leicester, sought desperately and unavailingly the favour of the Queen, and ultimately accepted a place in her service in Ireland, which meant banishment as virtually as a place in India would to-day. Henceforward his visits to London and the Court were few; sometimes a lover of travel would visit him in his house in Ireland as Raleigh did, but for the most he was left alone. It was in this atmosphere of loneliness and separation, hostile tribes pinning him in on every side, murder lurking in the woods and marshes round him, that he composed his greatest work. In it at last he died, on the heels of a sudden rising in which his house was burnt and his lands over-run by the wild Irish whom the tyranny of the English planters had driven to vengeance. Spenser was not without interest in his public duties; his *View of the State of Ireland* shows that. But it shows, too, that he brought to them singularly little sympathy or imagination. Throughout his tone is that of the worst kind of English officialdom; rigid subjection and in the last resort massacre are the remedies he would apply to Irish discontent. He would be a fine text—which might be enforced by modern examples—for a discourse on the evil effects of immersion in the government of a subject race upon men of letters. No man of action can be so consistently and cynically an advocate of brutalism as your man of letters. Spenser, of course, had his excuses; the problems of Ireland was new and it was something remote and difficult; in all but the mere distance for travel, Dublin was as far from London as Bombay is to-day. But to him and his like we must lay down partly the fact that to-day we have still and Irish problem.

But though fate and the necessity of a livelihood drove him to Ireland and the life of a colonist, poetry was his main business. He had been the centre of a brilliant set at Cambridge, one of those coteries whose fame, if they are brilliant and vivacious enough and have enough self-confidence, penetrates to the outer world before they leave the University. The thing happens in our own day, as the case of Oscar Wilde is witness; it happened in the case of Spenser; and when he and his friends Gabriel Harvey and Edward Kirke came "down" it was to immediate fame amongst amateurs of the arts. They corresponded with each other about literary matters, and Harvey published his part of the correspondence; they played like Du Bellay in France, with the idea of writing English verse in the quantitative measures of classical poetry; Spenser had a love affair in Yorkshire and wrote poetry about it, letting just enough be known to stimulate the imagination of the public. They tried their hand sat everything, imitated everything, and in all were brilliant, sparkling, and decorative; they got a kind of entrance to the circle of the Court. Then Spenser published his *Shepherd's Calendar*, a series of pastoral eclogues for every month of the year, after a manner taken from French and Italian pastoral writers, but coming ultimately from Vergil, and Edward Kirke furnished it with an elaborate prose commentary. Spenser took the same liberties with the pastoral form as did vergil himself; that is to say he used it as a vehicle for satire and allegory, made it carry political and social allusions, and planted in it references to his friends. By its publication Spenser became the first poet of the day. It was followed by some of his finest and most beautiful things—by the Platonic hymns, by the *Amoretti*, a series of sonnets inspired by his love for his wife; by the *Epithalamium*, on the occasion of his marriage to her; by *Mother Hubbard's Tale*, a satire written when despair at the coldness of the Queen and the enmity of Burleigh was beginning to take hold on the poet and endowed with a plainness and vigour foreign to most of his other work—and then by *The Fairy Queen*.

The poets of the Renaissance were not afraid of big things; every one of them had in his mind as the goal of poetic endeavour the idea of the heroic poem, aimed at doing for his own country what Vergil had intended to do for Rome in the *Æneid*, to celebrate it—its origin, its prowess, its greatness, and the causes of it, in epic verse. Milton, three-quarters of a century later, turned over in his mind the plan of an English epic on the wars of Arthur, and when he left it was only to forsake the singing of English origins for the more ultimate theme of the origins of mankind. Spenser designed to celebrate the character, the qualities and the training of the English gentleman. And because poetry, unlike philosophy, cannot deal with abstractions but must be vivid and concrete, he was forced to embody his virtues and foes to virtue and to use the way of allegory. His outward plan with its knights and dragons and desperate adventures, he procured from Ariosto. As for the use of allegory, it was one of the discoveries of the Middle Ages which the Renaissance condescended to retain. Spenser elaborated it beyond the wildest dreams of those students of Holy Writ who had first conceived it. His stories were to be interesting in themselves as tales of adventure, but within them they were to conceal an intricate treatment of the conflict of truth and falsehood in morals and religion. A character might typify at once Protestantism and England and Elizabeth and chastity and half the cardinal virtues, and it would have all the while the objective interest attaching to it as part of a story of adventure. All this must have made the poem difficult enough. Spenser's manner of writing it made it worse still. Once is familiar with the type of novel which only explains itself when the last chapter is reached—Stevenson's *Wrecker* is an example. *The Fairy Queen* was designed on somewhat the same plan. The last section was to relate and explain the unrelated and unexplained books which made up the poem, and at the court to which the separate knights of the separate books—the Red Cross Kinght and the rest—were to bring the fruit of their adventures, everything was to be made clear. Spenser did not live to finish his work; *The Fairy Queen*, like the *Æneid*, is an uncompleted poem and it is only from a prefatory letter to Sir

Walter Raleigh issued with the second published section that we know what the poem was intended to be. Had Spenser not published this explanation, it is impossible that anybody, even the acutest minded German professor, could have guessed.

The poem, as we have seen, was composed in Ireland, in the solitude of a colonists' plantation, and the author was shut off from his fellows while he wrote. The influence of his surroundings is visible in the writing. The elaboration of the theme would have been impossible or at least very unlikely if its author had not been thrown in on himself during its composition. Its intricacy and involution is the product of an over-concentration born of empty surroundings. It lacks vigour and rapidity; it winds itself into itself. The influence of Ireland, too, is visible in its landscapes, in its description of bogs and desolation, of dark forests in which lurk savages ready to spring out on those who are rash enough to wander within their confines. All the scenery in it which is not imaginary is Irish and not English scenery.

Its reception in England and at the Court was enthusiastic. Men and women read it eagerly and longed for the next section of *Pickwick*. The really liked it, really loved the intricacy and luxuriousness of it, the heavy exotic language, the thickly painted descriptions, the languorous melody of the verse. Mainly, perhaps, that was so because they were all either in wish or in deed poets themselves. Spenser has always been "the poets' poet." Milton loved him; so did Dryden, who said that Milton confessed to him that Spenser was "his original," a statement which has been pronounced incredible, but is, in truth, perfectly comprehensible, and most likely true. Pope admired him; Keats learned from him the best part of his music. You can trace echoes of him in Mr. Yeats. What is it that gives him this hold on him peers? Well, in the first place his defects do not detect from his purely poetic qualities. The story is impossibly told, but that will only worry those who are looking for a story. The allegory is hopelessly difficult; but as Hazlitt said "the allegory will not bite you"; you can let it alone. The crudeness and bigotry of Spenser's dealings with Catholicism, which are ridiculous when he pictures the monster Error vomiting books and pamphlets, and disgusting when he draws Mary Queen of Scots, do not hinder the pleasure of those who read him for his language and his art. He is great for other reasons than these. First because of the extraordinary smoothness and melody of his verse and the richness of his language—a golden diction that he drew from every source—new words, old words, obsolete words—such a mixture that the purist Ben Jonson remarked acidly that he wrote no language at all. Secondly because of the profusion of his imagery, and the extraordinarily keen sense for beauty and sweetness that went to its making. In an age of golden language and gallant imagery his was the most golden and the most gallant. And the language of poetry in England is richer and more varied than that in any other country in Europe to-day, because of what he did.

The Elizabethan Prose

Elizabethan prose brings us face to face with a difficulty which has to be met by every student of literature. Does the word "literature" cover every kind of writing ? Ought we to include in it writing that aims merely at instruction or is merely journey-work, as well as writing that has an artistic intention, or writing that, whether its author knew it or no, is artistic in its result ? Of course such a question causes us no sort of difficulty when it concerns itself only with what is being published to-day. We know very well that some things are literature and some merely journalism; that of novels, for instance, some deliberately intend to be works of art and others only to meet a passing desire for amusement or mental occupation. We know that most books serve or attempt to serve only a useful and not a literary purpose. But in reading the books of three centuries ago, unconsciously one's point of view shifts. Antiquity gilds journey-work; remoteness and quaintness of phrasing lend a kind of distinction to what are simply pamphlets or text-books that have been preserved by accident from the ephemeralness which was the common lot of hundreds of their fellows. One comes to regard as literature things that had no kind of literary value for their first audiences; to apply the same seriousness of judgment and the same tests to the pamphlets of Nash and Dekker as to the prose of Sidney and Bacon. One loses, in fact, that power to distinguish the important from the trivial which is one of the functions of a sound literary taste. Now, a study of the minor writing of the past is, of course, well worth a reader's pains. Pamphlets, chronicle histories, importance, they give us glimpses of the manners and habits and modes of thought of the day. They tell us more about the outward show of life than do the greater books. If you are interested in social history, they are the very thing. But the student of literature ought to beware of them, nor ought he to touch them till he is familiar with the big and lasting things. A man does not possess English literature if he knows what Dekker tells of the seven deadly sins of London and does not know the *Fairy Queen*. Though the wide and curious interest of the romantic critics of the nineteenth century found and illumined the byways of Elizabethan writing, the safest method of approach is the method of their predecessors —to keep hold on common sense, to look at literature, not historically as through the wrong end of a telescope, but closely and without a sense of intervening time, to know the best —the "classic"— and study it before the minor things.

In Elizabeth's reign, prose became for the first time, with cheapened printing, the common vehicle of amusement and information, and the books that remain to us cover many departments of writing. There are the historians who set down for us for the first time what they knew of the earlier history of England. There are the writers, like Harrison and Stubbs, who described the England of their own day, and there are many authors, mainly anonymous, who wrote down the accounts of the voyages of the discovers in the Western Seas. There are the novelists who translated Stories mainly from Italian sources. But of authors as conscious of a literary intention as the poets were, there are only two, Sidney and Lyly, and of authors who, though their first aim was hardly and artistic one, achieved an artistic result, only Hooker and the translators of the Bible. The Authorized Version of the Bible belongs strictly not to the reign of Elizabeth but to that of James, and we shall have to look at it when we come to discuss the seventeenth century. Hooker, in his book on Ecclesiastical Polity (an endeavour to set fourth and grounds of orthodox Anglicanism) employed a generous flowing, melodious style which has influenced many writers since and is familiar to us to-day in the copy of its used by Ruskin in his earlier works. Lyly and Sidney are worth looking at more closely.

The age was intoxicated with language. It went mad of a mere delight in words. Its writers were using a new tongue, for English was enriched beyond all recognition with borrowings from the ancient authors; and like and artists who become possessed of a new medium, they used it to excess. The early Elizabethans' use of the new prose was very like the use that educated Indians make of English to-day. It is not that these write it incorrectly, but only that they write too richly. And just as fuller use and knowledge teaches them spareness and economy and gives their writing simplicity and vigour, so seventeenth century practice taught Englishmen to write a more direct and undecorated style and gave us the smooth, simple, and vigorous writing of Dryden—the first really modern English prose. But the Elizabethans loved gaudier methods; they liked highly decorative modes of expression, in prose no less than in verse. The first author to give them these things was John Lyly, whose book *Euphues* was for the five or six years following it publication a fashionable craze that infected all society and gave its name to a peculiar and highly artificial style of writing that coloured the work of hosts of obscure and forgotten followers. Lyly wrote other things; his comedies may have taught Shakespeare the trick of *Love's Labour Lost;* be attempted a sequel of his most fainous work with better success than commonly attends sequels, but for us and for his own generation he is the author of one book. Everybody read it, everybody copied it. The maxims and sentences of advice for gentlemen which it contained were quoted and admired in the Court, where the author, though he never attained the lucrative position he hoped for, did what flattery could do to make a name for himself. The name "Euphuism" became a current description of an artificial way of using words that overflowed out of writing into speech and was in the mouth, while the vogue lasted, of everybody who was anybody in the circle that fluttered round the Queen.

The style of *Euphues* was parodied by Shakespeare and many attempts have been made to imitate it since. Most of them are inaccurate—Sir Walter Scott's wild attempt the most inaccurate of all. They fail because their authors have imagined that "Euphuism" is simply a highly artificial and "flowery" way of talking. As a matter of fact it is made up of a very exact and very definite series of parts. The writing is done on a plan which has three main characteristics as follows. First, the structure of the sentence is based on antithesis and alliteration; that is to say, it falls into equal parts similar in sound but with a different sense; for example, Euphues is described as a young gallant "of more wit than wealth, yet of more wealth than wisdom." All the characters in the book, which is roughly in the form of a novel, speak in this way, sometimes in sentences long drawn out which are oppressively monotonous and tedious, and sometimes shortly with a certain approach to epigram. The second characteristic of the style is the reference of every stated fact to some classical authority, that is to say, the author cannot mention friendship without quoting David and Jonathan, nor can lovers in his book accuse each other of faithlessness without quoting the instance of Cressida or Aeneas. This appeal to classical authority and wealth of classical allusion is used to decorate pages which deal with matters of every-day experience. Seneca, for instance, is quoted as reporting "that too much bending breaketh the bow," a fact which might reasonably have been supposed to be known to the author himself. This particular form of writing perhaps influenced those who copied Lyly more than anything else in his book. It is a fashion of the more artificial kind of Elizabethan writing in all schools to employ a wealth of classical allusion. Even the simple narratives in *Hakluyt's Voyages* are not free from it, and one may hardly hope to read an account of a voyage to the Indies without stumbling on a preliminary reference to the opinions of Aristotle and Plato. Lastly, *Euphues* is characterised by an extraordinary wealth of allusion to natural history, mostly of a fabulous kind. "I have read that the bull being tied to the fig tree loseth his tail; that the whole herd of deer stand at gaze if they smell a sweet apple; that the dolphin after the sound of music is brought to the shore," and so on. His book is full of these things, and the style weakens and loses its force because of them.

Of course there is much more in his book than this outward decoration. He wrote with the avowed purpose of instructing courtiers and gentlemen how to live. *Euphues* is full of grave reflections and weighty morals, and is indeed a collection of essays on education, on friendship, on religion and philosophy, and on the favourite occupation and curriculum of Elizabethan youth—foreign travel. The fashions and customs of his countrymen which he condemns in the course of his teaching are the same as those inveighed against by Stubbs and other contemporaries. He disliked manners and fashions copied from Italy; particularly he disliked the extravagant fashions of women. One woman only escapes his censure, and she, of course, is the Queen, whom Euphues and his companion in the book come to England to see. In the main the teaching of Euphues inculcates a humane and liberal, if not very profound creed, and the book shares with *The Fairy Queen* the honour of the earlier Puritanism—the Puritanism that besides the New Testament had the *Republic*.

But Euphues, though he was in his time the popular idol, was not long in finding a successful rival. Seven years before his death Sir Philip Sidney, in a period of retirement from the Court wrote "*The Countess of Pembroke's Arcadia*"; it was published ten years after it had been composed. The *Arcadia* is the first English example of the prose pastoral romance, as the *Shepherd's Calendar* is of our pastoral verse. Imitative essays in its style kept appearing for two hundred years after it, till Wordsworth and other poets who knew the country drove its unrealities out of literature. The aim of it and of the school to which it belonged abroad was to find a setting for a story which should leave the author perfectly free to plant in it any improbability he liked, and to do what he liked with the relations of his characters. In the shade of beech trees, the coils of elaborated and intricate love-making wind and unravel themselves through an endless afternoon. In that art nothing is too far-fetched, nothing too sentimental, no sorrow too unreal. The pastoral romance was used, too, to cover other things besides a sentimental and decorative treatment of love. Authors wrapped up as shepherds their political friends and enemies, and the pastoral eclogues in verse which Spenser and others composed are full of personal and political allusion. Sidney's story carries no politics and he depends for its interest solely on the wealth of differing episodes and the stories and arguments of love which it contains. The story would furnish plot enough for twenty ordinary novels, but probably those who read it when it was published were attracted by other things than the march of its incidents. Certainly no one could read it for the plot now. Its attraction is mainly one of style. It goes, you feel, one degree beyond *Euphues* in the direction of freedom and poetry. And just because of this greater freedom, its characteristics are much less easy to fix than those of *Euphues*. Perhaps its chief quality is best described as that of exhaustiveness. Sidney will take a word and toss it to and fro in a page till its meaning is sucked dry and more than sucked dry. On page after page the same trick is employed, often in some new and charming way, but with the inevitable effect of wearying the reader, who tries to do the unwisest of all things with a book of this kind—to read on. This trick of bandying words is, of course, common in Shakespeare. Other marks of Sidney's style belong similarly to poetry rather than to prose. Chief of them is what Ruskin christened the "pathetic fallacy" — the assumption (not common in his day) which connects the appearance of nature with the moods of the artist who looks at it, or demands such a connection. In its day the *Arcadia* was hailed as a reformation by men nauseated by the rhythmical patterns of Lyly. A modern reader finds himself confronting it in something of the spirit that he would confront the prose romances, say, of William Morris, finding it charming as a poet's essay in prose but no more: not to be ranked with the highest.

The Drama

Biologists tell us that the hybrid—the product of a variety of ancestral stocks—is more fertile than an organism with a direct and unmixed ancestry; perhaps the analogy is not too fanciful as the starting-point of a study of Elizabethan drama, which owed its strength and vitality, more than to anything else, to the variety of the discordant and contradictory elements of which it was made up. The drama was the form into which were moulded the thoughts and desires of the best spirits of the time. It was the flower of the age. To appreciate its many-sided significance and achievements it is necessary to disentangle carefully its roots, in religion, in the revival of the classics, in popular entertainments, in imports from abroad, in the air of enterprise and adventure which belonged to the time.

As in Greece, drama in England was in its beginning a religious thing. Its oldest continuous tradition was from the mediaeval Church. Early in the Middle ages the clergy and their parishioners began the habit, at Christmas, Ester and other holy days, of playing some part of the story of Christ's life suitable to the festival of the day. These plays were liturical, and originally, no doubt, overshadowed by a choral element. But gradually the inherent human capacity for mimicry and drama took the upper hand; from ceremonies they developed into performances; they passed from the stage in the church porch to the stage in the street. A waggon, the natural human platform for mimicry or oratory, because in England as it was in Greece, the cradle of the drama. This momentous change in the history of the miracle play, which made it in all but its occasion and its subject a secular thing, took place about the end of the twelfth century. The rise of the town guilds gave the plays a new character; the friendly rivalry of leagued craftsmen elaborated their production; and at length elaborate cycles were founded which were performed at Whitsuntide, beginning at sunrise and lasting all through the day right on to dusk. Each town had its own cycle, and of these the cycles of York, Wakefield, Chester and Coventry still remain. So too, does an eye-witness's account of a Chester performance where the plays took place yearly on three days, beginning with Whit Monday. "The manner of these plays were, every company had his pageant or part, a high scaffold with two rooms, a higher and a lower, upon four wheels. In the lower they apparelled themselves and in the higher room they played, being all open on the top that all beholders might hear and see them. They began first at the abbey gates, and when the first pageant was played, it was wheeled to the high cross before the mayor and so to every street. So every street had a pageant playing upon it at one tome, till all the pageants for the day appointed were played." The "companies" were the town guilds and the several "pageants" different scenes in Old or New Testament story. As far as was possible each company took for its pageant some Bible story fitting to its trade; in York the goldsmiths played the three Kings of the East bringing precious gifts, the fishmongers, the flood, and the shipwrights the building of Noah's ark. The tone of these plays was not reverent; reverence after all implies near at hand its opposite in unbelief. But they were realistic and they contained within them the seeds of later drama in the aptitude with which they grafted into the scared story pastoral and city manners taken straight from life. The shepherds who watched by night at Bethlehem where real English shepherds furnished with boisterous and realistic comic relief. Noah was a real shipwright.

"It shall be clinched each ilk and deal.
Withe nails that are both noble and new
Thus shall I fix it to the keel,
Take here a rivet and there a screw,
With there bow there now, work I well,
This work, I warrant, both good and true."

Cain and Abel were English farmers just as truly as Bottom and his fellows were English craftsmen. But then Julius Caesar has a doublet and in Dutch pictures the apostles wear broad-brimmed hats. Squeamishness about historical accuracy is of a later date, and when it came we gained in correctness less than we lost in art.

The miracle plays, then, are the oldest antecedent of Elizabethan drama, but it must not be supposed they were over and done with before the great age began. The description of the Chester performances, part of which has been quoted, was written in 1594. Shakespeare must, one would think, have seen the Coventry cycle; at any rate he was familiar, as every one of the time must have been, with the performances; "Out -heroding Herod" bears witness to that. One must conceive the development of the Elizabethan age as something so rapid in its accessibility to new impressions and new manners and learning and modes of thought that for years the old and now subsisted side by side. Think of modern Japan, a welter of old faiths and crafts and ideals and inrushing Western civilization all mixed up and side by side in the strangest contrasts and you will understand what it was. The miracle plays stayed on beside Marlowe and Shakespeare till Puritanism frowned upon them. But when the end came it came quickly. The last recorded performance took place in London when King James entertained Gondomar, the Spanish ambassador. And perhaps we should regard that as a "command" performance, reviving as command performances commonly do, something dead for a generation—in this case, purely out of compliment to the faith and inclination of a distinguished guest.

Next in order of development after the miracle or mystery plays, though contemporary in their popularity, came what we called "moralities" or "moral interludes" —pieces designed to enforce a religious or ethical lesson and perhaps to get back into drama something of the edification which realism had ousted from the miracles. They dealt in allegorical and figurative personages, expounded wise saws and moral lessons, and squared rather with the careful self-concern of the newly established Protestantism than with the frank and joyous jest in life which was more characteristic of the time. *Everyman*, the oftenest revived and best known of them, if not the best, is very typical of the class. They had their influences, less profound than that of the miracles, on the full drama. It is said the "Vice"—unregeneracy commonly degenerated into comic relief—is the ancestor of the fool in Shakespeare, but more likely both are successive creations of a dynasty of actors who practised the unchanging and immemorial art of the clown. The general structure of *Everyman* and some of its fellows, heightened and made more dramatic, gave us Marlowe's *Faustus*. There perhaps the influence ends.

The rise of a professional class of actors brought one step nearer the full growth of drama. Companies of strolling players formed themselves and passed from town to town, seeking like the industrious amateurs of the guilds, civic patronage, and performing in town-halls, market-place booths, or inn yards, whichever served them best. The structure of the Elizabethan inn yard (you may see some survivals still, and there are the pictures in *Pickwick*) was very favourable for their purpose. The galleries round it made seats like our boxes and circle for the more privileged spectators; in the centre on the floor of the yard stood the crowd or sat, if they had stools with them. The stage was a platform set on this floor space with its back against one side of the yard, where perhaps one of the inn-room served as a dressing room. So suitable was this "fit-up" as actors call it, that when theatres came to be build in London they were built on the inn-yard pattern. All the playhouses of the bankside from the "Curtain" to the "Globe" were square or circular places with galleries rising above one another three parts round, a floor space of beaten earth open to the sky in the middle, and jutting out one to it a platform stage with a tiring room capped by a gallery behind it.

The entertainment given by these companies of players (who usually got the patronage and took the title of some lord) was various. They played moralities and interludes, they played formless chronicle history plays like the *Troublesome Reign of King John*, on which Shakespeare worked for his king John: but above and before all they were each a company of specialists, every one of whom had his own talent and performance for which he was admired. The Elizabethan stage was the ancestor of our music-hall, and to the modern music-hall rather than to the theatre it bears its affinity. If you wish to realize the aspect of the Globe or the Black-friars it is to a lower class music-hall, and to the modern music-hall rather than to the theatre it bears its affinity. If you wish to realize the aspect of the Globe or the Black-friars it is to a lower class music-hall you must go. The quality of the audience is a point of agreement. The Globe was frequented by young "bloods" by the more disreputable portions of the community, racing men (or their equivalents of that day) "coney catchers" and the like; commonly the only women present were women of the town. The similarity extends from the auditorium to the stage. The Elizabethan playgoer delighted in virtuosity; in exhibitions of strength or skill from his actors; the broadsword combat in *Macbeth*, and the wrestling in *As Ycu Like It*, were real trails of skill. The bear in the *Winter's Tale* was no doubt a real bear got from a bear pit, near by in the bankside. The comic actors especially were the very grandfathers of our music-hall stars; Tarleton and Kemp and Cowley, the chief of them, were as much popular favourites and esteemed as separate from the plays they played in as is Harry Lauder. Their songs and tunes were printed and sold in hundreds as broadsheets, just as pirated music-hall songs are sold to-day. This is to be noted because it explains a great deal in the subsequent evolution of the drama. It explains the delight in having everything represented actually on the stage, all murders, battles, duels. It explains the magnificent largesse given by Shakespeare to the professional fool. Work had to be found for him, and Shakespeare, whose difficulties were stepping-stones to his triumphs, gave him Touchstone and Feste, the Porter in *Macbeth* and the Fool in *Lear*. Others met the problem in an attitude of frank despair. Not all great tragic writers can easily or gracefully wield the pen of comedy, and Marlowe in *Dr. Faustus* took the course of leaving the low comedy which the audience loved and a high salaried actor demanded, to an inferior collaborator.

Alongside this drama of street platforms and inn-yards and public theatres, there grew another which, blending with it, produced the Elizabethan drama which we know. The public theatres were not the only places at which plays were produced. At the University, at the Inns of Court (which then more than now, were besides centres of study rather exclusive and expensive clubs), and at the court they were an important part of almost every festival. At these places were produced academic compositions, either allegorical like the mosques, copies of which we find in Shakespeare and by Ben Jonson, or comedies modelled on Seneca. The last were incomparably the most important. The Elizabethan age, which always thought of literature as a guide or handmaid to life, was naturally attracted to a poet who dealt in maxims and "sentences"; his rhetoric appealed to men for whom words and great passages of verse were an intoxication that only a few to-day can understand or sympathize with; his bloodthirstiness and gloom to an age so full-blooded as not to shrink from horrors. Tragedies early began to be written on the strictly, Senecan model, and generally, like Seneca's, with some ulterior intention. Sackville's *Gorboduc*, the first tragedy in English, produced at a great festival at the Inner Temple, aimed at inducing Elizabeth to marry and save the miseries of a disputed succession. To be put to such a use argues the importance and dignity of this classical tragedy of the learned societies and the court. None of the pieces composed in this style were written for the popular theatre, and indeed they could not have been a success on it. The Elizabethan audience, as we have seen, loved action, and in these Senecan tragedies the action took place "off." But they had a strong and abiding influence on the popular stage; they gave it its ghosts, its supernatural warnings, its conception of nemesis and revenge, they gave it its love of introspection and the long passages in which introspection, description or reflection, either in soliloquy or dialogue, holds up he action; contradictorily enough they gave it somethings at least of its melodrama. Perhaps they helped to enforce the lesson of the miracle plays that a dramatist's proper business was elaboration rather than invention. None of the Elizabethans dramatists except Ben Jonson habitually constructed their own plots. Their method was to take something ready at their hands and overlay it with realism or poetry or romance. The stories of their plays, like that of Hamlet's Mousetrap, were "extant and write in choice Italian," and very often their methods of preparation were very like his.

Something of the way in which the spirit of adventure of the time affected and finished the drama we have already seen. It is time now to turn to the dramatists themselves.

Of Marlowe, Kyd, Greene, and Peele, the "University Wits" who fused the academic and the popular drama, and by giving the latter a sense of literature and learning to mould it to finer issues, gave us Shakespeare, only Marlowe can be treated here. Greene and Peele, the former by his comedies, the latter by his historical plays, and Kyd by his tragedies, have their places in the text-books, but they belong to a secondary order of dramatic talent. Marlowe ranks amongst the greatest. It is not merely that historically he is the head and fount of the whole movement, that he changed blank verse, which had been a lumbering instrument before him, into something rich and ringing and rapid and made it the vehicle for the greatest English poetry after him. Historical relations apart, he is great in himself. More than any other English writer of any age, except Byron, he symbolizes the youth of his time: its hotbloodeness, its lust after knowledge and power and life inspires all his pages. The teaching of Machavelli, misunderstood for their own purposes by would-be imitators, furnished the reign of Elizabeth with the only political ideals it possessed. The simple brutalism of the creed, with means justified by ends and the unbridled self-regarding pursuit of power, attracted men for whom the Spanish monarchy and the Struggle to overthrow it were the main factors and polities. Marlowe took it and turned it to his own uses. There is in his writings a lust of power, "a hunger and thirst after unrighteousness," a glow of the imagination unhallowed by anything nut its own energy which is in the spirit of the time. In *Tamburlaine* it is the power of conquest, stirred by and reflecting, as we have seen, the great deeds of his day. In *Dr. Faustus* it is the pride of will and eagerness of curiosity. Faustus is devoured by a tormenting desire to enlarge his knowledge to the utmost bounds of nature and art and to extend his power with his knowledge. His is the spirit of Renaissance scholarship heightened to a passionate excess. The play gleams with the pride of learning and a knowledge which learning brings, and with the names is that comes after it. "Oh! gentlemen! hear me with patience and tremble not at my speeches. Though my heart pant and quiver to remember that I have been a student here these thirty years; oh! I would I had never seen Wittemburg, never read book!" And after the agonizing struggle in which Faustus's soul is torn from him to hell, learning comes in at the quiet close.

" Yet, for he was a scholar once admired,
For wondrous knowledge in our German Schools;
We'll give his mangled limbs due burial;
And all the students, clothed in morning black
Shall wait upon his heavy funeral."

Some one character is a centre of overmastering pride and ambition in every play. In the *Jew of Malta* it is the hero Barabbas. In *Edward II.* it is Piers Gaveston. In *Edward II* indeed, two elements are mixed—the element of Machiavelli and Tamburlaine in Gaveston, and the purely tragic element which evolves from within itself the style in which it shall be treated, in the King. "The reluctant pangs of abdicating Royalty," wrote Charles Lamb in a famous passage, "furnished hints which Shakespeare scarcely improved in his *Richard II.*; and the death scene of Marlowe's King moves pity and terror beyond any scene, ancient or modern, with which I am acquainted." Perhaps the play gives the hint of what Marlowe might have become had not the dagger of a groom in a tavern cut short at thirty his burning career.

Even in that time of romance and daring speculation he went further than his fellows. He was said to have been tainted with atheism, to have denied God and the Trinity; had he lived he might have had trouble with the Star Chamber. The free-voyaging intellect of the age found this one way of outlet, but if literary evidences are to be trusted sixteenth and seventeenth century atheism was a very crude business. The *Atheist's Tragedy* of Tourneur (a dramatist who need not otherwise detain us) given some measure of its intelligence and depth. Says the villain to the heroine,

> "No? Then invoke
> Your great supposed Protector. I will do't."

to which she:

> "Supposed Protector! Are you an atheist, then
> I know my fears and prayers are spent in vain."

Marlowe's very faults and extravagances, and they are many, are only the obverse of his greatness. Magnitude and splendor of language when the thought is too shrunken to fill it out, becomes mere inflation. He was a butt of the parodists of the day. And Shakespeare, though he honoured him "on this side idolatry," did his share of ridicule. Ancient Pistol is fed and stuffed with relics and rags of Marlowesque affection—

> "Holla! ye pampered jades of Asia.
> Can ye not draw nut twenty miles a day."

is a quotation taken straight from *Tamburlaine.*

A study of Shakespeare, who refuses to be crushed within the limits of a general essay, is no part of the plan of this book. We must take up the story of the drama with the reign of James and with the contemporaries of his later period, though of course, a treatment which is conditioned by the order of development is not strictly chronological, and some of the plays we shall have to refer to belong to the close of the sixteenth century. We are apt to forget that alongside Shakespeare and at his heels other dramatists were supplying material for the theatre. The influence of Marlowe and particularly of Kyd, whose *Spanish Tragedy* with its crude mechanism of ghosts and madness and revenge caught the popular taste, worked itself out in a score of journeymen dramatists, mere hack writers, who turned their hand to plays as the hacks of to-day turn their hand to novels, and with no more literary merit than that caught as an echo from better men than themselves. One of the worst of these—he is also one of the most typical— was John Marston, a purveyor of tragic gloom and sardonic satire, and an impostor in both, whose tragedy *Antonia and Mellida* was published in the same year as Shakespeare's *Hamlet*. Both plays owed their style and plot to the same tradition—the tradition created by Kyd's *Spanish Tragedy* —in which ghostly promptings to revenge, terrible crime, and a feigned madman waiting his opportunity are the elements of tragedy. Nothing could be more fruitful in an understanding of the relations of Shakespeare to his age than a comparison of the two. The style of *Antonio and Mellida* is the style of *The Murder of Gonzago*. There is no subtlety nor introspection, the pale cast of thought falls with no shadow over its scenes. And it is typical of a score of plays of the kind we have and beyond doubt of hundreds that have perished. Shakespeare stands alone.

Beside this journey-work tragedy of revenge and murder which had its root through Kyd and Marlowe in Seneca and in Italian romance, there was a journey-work comedy of low life made up of loosely constructed strings of incidents, buffoonery and romance, that had its roots in a joyous and fantastic study of the common people. These plays are happy and high-spirited and, compared with the ordinary run of the tragedies, or better work-manship. They deal in the familiar situations of low comedy—the clown, the thrifty citizen and his frivolous wife, the gallant, the bawd, the good apprentice and the bad portrayed vigorously and tersely and with a careless kindly gaiety that still charms in the reading. The best writers in this kind were Middleton and Dekker—and the best play to read as a sample of it *Eastward Ho!* in which Marston put off his affectation of sardonical melancholy and joined with Jonson and Dekker to produce what is the masterpiece of the non-Shakespearean comedy of the time.

For all our habit of grouping their works together it is a far cry in spirit and temperament from the dramatists whose heyday was under Elizabeth and those who reached their prime under her successor. Quickly though insensibly the temper of the nation suffered eclipse. The high hopes and the ardency of the reign of Elizabeth saddened into a profound pessimism and gloom in that of James. This apparition of unsought melancholy has been widely noted and generally assumed to be inexplicable. In broad outline its causes are clear enough. "To travel hopefully is a better thing than to arrive." The Elizabethans were, if ever any were, hopeful travellers. The winds blew them to the four quarters of the world, they navigated all seas; they sacked rich cities. They beat off the great Armada, and harried the very coasts of Spain. They pushed discovery to the ends of the world and amassed great wealth. Under James all these things were over. Please was made with Spain: national pride was wounded by the solicitous anxiety of the King for a Spanish marriage for the heir to the throne. Sir Walter Raleigh, a romantic adventure lingering beyond his time, was beheaded out of hand by the ungenerous timidity of the monarch of whom had been transferred devotion and loyalty he was unfitted to receive. The Court which had been a center of flashing and gleaming brilliance degenerated into a knot of sycophants humouring the pragmatic and self-important folly of a king in whom had implanted themselves all the vices of the Scots and none of their virtues. Nothing seemed left remarkable beneath the visiting moon. The bright day was done and they were for the dark. The uprising of Puritanism and the shadow of impending religious strife darkened the temper of the time.

The change affected all literature and particularly the drama, which because it appeals to what all men have in common, commonly reflects soonest a change in the outlook or spirits of a people. The onslaughts of the dramatists on the theatre, became more virulent and evenomed. What a difference between the sunny satire of Sir Andrew Aguecheek and the dark animosity of The *Atheists' Tragedy* with its Languebeau Snuffe ready to carry out any villainy proposed to him! "I speak sir," says a lady in the same play to a courtier who played with her in an attempt to carry on a quick witted, "conceited" love passage in the vein of *Much Ado*. "I speak, sir, as the fashion now is, in earnest," The quick-witted, light-hearted age was gone. It is natural that tragedy reflected this melancholy in its deepest from Gloom deepened and had no light to behave it, men supped full of horrors —there was no slackening of the tension, no concession to overwrought nerves, no resting-place for the overwrought soul. It is in the dramatist John Webster that this new spirit has its most powerful exponent.

The influence of machiavelli, which had given Marlowe tragic figures that were bright and splendid and burning, smouldered in Webster into a duskier and intenser heat. His fame rests on two tragedies, The *White Devil* and *The Duchess of Malfi*. Both are stories of lust and crime, full of hate and hideous vengeance, and through each runs a vein of bitter and ironical comment on men and women. In them chance plays the part of fate, "Blind accident and blundering mishap—'such a mistake,' says one of the criminals, 'as I have often seen in a play' are the steersmen of their fortunes and the doomsmen of their deeds." His characters are gloomy; meditative and philosophic murderers, cynical informers, sad and loving women, and they are all themselves in every phrase that they utter. But they are studied in earnestness and sincerity. Unquestionably he is the greatest of Shakespeare's successors in the romantic drama, perhaps his only direct imitiator. He has single lines worthy to set beside those in *Othello* or *King Lear*. His dirge in the *Duchess of Malfi*, Charles Lamb thought worthy to be set beside the ditty in *The Tempest*, which reminds Ferdinand of his drowned father. "As that is of the water, watery, so this is of the earth, earthy." He has earned his place among the greatest of our dramatists by his two plays, the theme of which matched his sombre genius and the somberness of the season in which it flowered.

But the drama could not survive long the altered times, and the voluminous plays of Beaumont and Fletcher mark the beginning of the end. They are the decadence of Elizabethan drama. Decadence is a term often used loosely and therefore hard to define, but we may say broadly that an art is decadent when any particular one of the elements which go to its making occurs in excess and disturbs the balance of forces which keeps the work a coherent and intact whole. Poetry is decadent when the sound is allowed to outrun the sense or when the suggestions, say, of colour, which it contains are allowed to crowd out its deeper implications. Thus we can call such a poem as this one well-known of O'Shaughnessy's

> " We are the music-makers,
> We are the dreamers of dreams."

decadent because it conveys nothing but the mere delight in an obvious rhythm of words, or such a poem as Morris's "Two red roses across the moon," because a meaningless refrain, merely pleasing in tis word texture, breaks in at intervals on the reader. The drama of Beaumont and Fletcher in decadent tin two ways. In the first place those variations and licences with which Shakespeare in his later plays diversified the blank verse handed on to him by Marlowe, they use without any restraint or measure. "Weak" endings and "double" endings, i.e. lines which end either on a conjunction or proposition or some other unstressed word, or lines in which there is a syllable too many—abound in their plays. They destroyed blank verse as a musical and resonant poetic instrument by letting this elements of variety outrun the sparing and skilful use which alone could justify it. But they were decadent in other and deeper ways than that. Sentiment in their plays usurps the place of character. Eloquent and moving speeches and fine figures are not longer subservient to the presentation of character in action, but are set down for their own sake, "What strange self-trumpetrs and tongue-bullies all the brave soldiers of Beaumont and Fletcher are," said Coleridge. When they die they die to the music of their own virtue. When dreadful deeds are done they are described not with that authentic and lurid vividness which throws light on the working of the human heart in Shakespeare or Webster but in tedious rhetoric. Resignation, not fortitude, is the authors' forte and they play upon it amazingly. The sterner tones of their predecessors melt into the long drawn broken accent of pathos and woe. This delight not in action or in emotion arising from action but in passivity of suffering is only one aspect of a certain mental flaccidity in grain. Shakespeare may be free and even coarse. Beaumont and Fletcher cultivate indecency. They made their subject not their master but their plaything, or an occasion for the convenient exercise of their own powers of figure and rhetoric.

Of their followers, Massinger, Ford and Shirley, no more need be said than they carried one step further the faults of their masters. Emotion and tragic passion give way to wire-drawn sentiment. Tragedy takes on the air of a masquerade.

Puritans' closing of the theatre only gave it a *coup de grace*. In England it has had no second birth.

Outside the direct romantic succession there worked another author whose lack of sympathy with it, as well as his close connection with the age which followed, justifies his separate treatment. Ben Jonson shows a marked contrast to Shakespeare in his character, his accomplishments, and his attitude to letters, while his career was more varied than Shakespeare's own. The first "classic" in English writing, he was a "romantic" in action. In his adventurous youth he was by turns scholar, soldier, bricklayer, actor. He trailed a pike with Leicester in the Low Countries; on his return to England fought a duel and killed his man, only escaping hanging by benefit of clergy; at the end of his life he was Poet laureate. Such a career is sufficiently diversified, and it forms a striking contrast to the plainness and severity of his work. But it must not lead us to forget or under-estimate his learning and knowledge. Not Gray nor Tennyson, nor Swindburne—perhaps not even Milton—was a better scholar. He is one of the earliest of English writers to hold and express different theories about literature. He consciously appointed himself a teacher; was a missionary of literature with a definite creed.

But through in a general way his dramatic principles are opposed to the romantic tendencies of his age, he is by no means blindly classical. He never consented to be bound by the "Unities"—that conception of dramatic construction evolved out of Aristotle and Horace and elaborated in the Renaissance till, in its strictest from, it laid down that the whole scene of a play should be in one place, its whole action deal with one single series of events, and the time it represented as elapsing be no greater than the time it took in playing. He was always pre-eminently an Englishman of his own day with a scholar's rather than a poet's temper, hating extravagance, hating bombast and cant, and only limited because in ruling out these things he ruled out much else that was essential to the spirit of the time. As a craftsman he was uncompromising; he never bowed to the tastes of the public and never veiled his scorn of those—Shakespeare among them— whom he conceived to do so; but he knew and valued his own work, as his famous last word to an audience who might be unsympathetic stands to witness,

"By God 'tis good, and if you like it you may."

Compare the temper it reveals with the titles of the two contemporary comedies of his gentler and greater brother, the one *As You Like It*, the other *What You Will*. Of the two attitudes towards the public, and they might stand as typical of tow kinds of artists, neither perhaps can claim complete sincerity. A truculent and noisy disclaimer of their favours is not a bad tone to assume towards an audience; in the end it is apt to succeed as well as the sub-ironical compliance which is its opposite.

Jonson's theory of comedy and the consciousness with which he set it against the practice of his contemporaries and particularly of Shakespeare receive explicit statement in the prologue to *Every Man Out of His Humour*—one of his earlier plays. "I travail with another objection, Signor, which I fear will be enforced against the author ere I can be delivered of it," says Mitis. "What's that, sir? " replies Cordatus. Mitis:—"That the argument of his comedy might have bene of some other nature, as of a duke to be in love with a countess, and that countess to be in love with the duke's son, and the son to love the lady's waiting maid; some such cross-wooing, better than to be thus near and familiarly allied to the times." Cordatus: "You say well, but I would fain hear one of these autumn judgements define *Quin sit comœdia* ? If he cannot, let him concern himself with Cicero's definition, till he have strength to propose to himself a better, who would have a comedy to be *invitatio vitœ speculum consuetudinis, imago veritatis*; a thing throughout pleasant and ridiculous and accommodated to the correction of manners." That was what he meant his comedy to be, and so he conceived the popular comedy of the day. *Twelfth Night* and *Much Ado*. Shakespeare might play with dukes and countesses, serving-women and pages, clowns and disguises; he would come down more near and ally himself familiarly with the times. So comedy was to be medicinal, to purge contemporary London of its follies and its sins; and it was to be constructed with regularity and elaboration, respectful to the Unities if not ruled by them, and build up of characters each the embodiment of some "humour" or eccentricity, and each when his eccentricity is displaying itself at its fullest, outwitted and exposed. This conception of "humours," based on a physiology which was already obsolescent, takes heavily from the realism of Jonson's methods, nor does his use of a careful vocabulary of contemporary colloquialism and slang save him from a certain dryness and tediousness to modern readers. The truth is he was less a satirist of contemporary manners than a satirist in the abstract who followed the models of classical writers in this style, and he found the vices and follies of his own day hardly adequate to the intricacy and elaborateness of the plots which he constructed for their exposure. At the first glance his people are contemporary types, at the second they betray themselves for what they are really—cock-shies setup by the new comedy of Greece that every "classical" satirist in Rome or France or England has had his shot at since. One wonders whether Ben Jonson, for all his satirical intention, had as much observation—as much of an eye for contemporary types—as Shakespeare's rusties and roysterers prove him to have had. It follows that all but one or two of his plays, when they are put on the stage to-day are apt to come to one with a sense of remoteness and other-worldliness which we hardly feel with Shakespeare or Molière. His muse moves along the high-road of comedy which is the Roman road, and she caries in her train types that have done service to many since the ancients fashioned them years ago. Jealous husbands, foolish pragmatic fathers, a dissolute son, a boastful soldier, a cunning slave—they all are merely counters by which the game of comedy used to be played. In England, since Shakespeare took his hold on the stage, that road has been stopped for us, that game has ceased to amuse.

Ben Jonson, then in a certain degree filed in him intention. Had he kept closer to contemporary life, instead of merely grafting on to it types he had learned from books, he might have made himself an English Moliere —without Moliere's breadth and clarity—but with a corresponding vigour and strength which would have kept his work sweet. And he might have founded a school of comedy that would have got its roots deeper into our national life than the trivial and licentious Restoration comedy ever succeeded in doing. As it is, his importance is mostly hysterical. One must credit him with being the first of the English classics—of the age which gave us Dryden and Swift and Pope. Perhaps that is enough in his praise.

The 17th Century

With the seventeenth century the great school of imaginative writers that made glorious the last years of Elizabeth's reign, had passed away. Spenser was dead before 1600, Sir Philip Sidney a dozen years earlier, and though Shakespeare and Dryton and many other men whom we class roughly as Elizabethan lived on to work under James, their temper and their ideals belong to the earlier day. The seventeenth century, not in England only but in Europe, brought a new way of thinking with it, and gave a new direction to human interest and to human affairs. It is not perhaps easy to define nor is it visible in the greater writers of the time. Milton, for instance, and Sir Thomas Browne are both of them too big, and in their genius too far separated from their fellows to give us much clue to altered conditions. It is commonly in the work of lesser and forgotten writers that the spirit of an age has its fullest expression. Genius is a law to itself; it moves in another dimension; it is out of time. To define this seventeenth century spirit, then, one must look at the literature of the age as a whole. What is there that one finds in it which marks a change in temperament and outlook from the Renaissance, and the time which immediately followed it?

Putting it very broadly one may say that literature in the seventeenth century becomes for the first time essential modern inspirit. We began our survey of modern English literature at the Renaissance because the discovery of the New World, and the widening of human experience and knowledge, which that and the revival of classical learning implied, mark a definite break from a way of thought which had been continuous since the break up of the Roman Empire. The men of the Renaissance felt themselves to be modern. They started afresh, owing nothing to their immediate forbears, and when they talked, say, of Chaucer, they did so in very much the same accent as we do to-day. He was mediaeval and obsolete; the interest which he possessed was a purely literary interest; his readers did not meet him easily on the same plane of thought, or forget the lapse of time which separated him from them. And in another way too, the Renaissance began Modern writing. Inflections had bene dropped. The revival of the classics had enriched our vocabulary, and the English language, after a gradual impoverishment which followed the obsolescence one after another of the local dialects, attained a fairly fixed from. There is more difference between the language of the English writings of Sir Thomas More and that of the prose of Chaucer than there is between that of More and of Ruskin. But it is not till the seventeenth century that the modern spirit, in the fullest sense of the word, comes into being. Defined it means a spirit of observation, of preoccupation with detail, of stress laid on matter of fact, of analysis of feelings and mental processes, of free argument upon institutions and government. In relation to knowledge, it is the spirit of science, and the study of science, which is the essential intellectual fact in modern history, dates from just this time, from Bacon and Newton and Descartes. In relation to literature, it is the spirit of criticism, and criticism in England is the creation of the seventeenth century. The positive temper, the attitude of realism, is everywhere in the as ascendant. The sixteenth century made voyages of discovery; the seventeenth sat down to take stock of the riches it had gathered. For the first time in English literature writing becomes a vehicle for storing and conveying facts.

It would be easy to give instances: one must suffice here. Biography, which is one of the most characteristic kinds of English writing, was unknown to the moderns as late as the sixteenth century. Partly the awakened interest in the careers of the ancient statesmen and soldiers which the study of Plutarch had excited, and partly the general interest in, and craving for, facts set men writing down the lives of their fellows. The earliest English biographies date from this time. In the beginning they were concerned, like Plutarch, with men of action, and when Sir Fulke Greville wrote a brief account of his friend Sir Philip Sidney it was the courtier and the soldier, and not the author, that he designed to celebrate. But some men of letters came within their scope, and though the interest in the lives of authors came too late to give as the contemporary life of Shakespeare we so much long for, it was early enough to make possible those masterpieces of condensed biography in which Isaak Walton celebrates Herbert and Donne. Fuller and Aubrey, to name only two authors, spent lives of laborious industry two hunting down and chronicling the smallest facts about the worthies of their day and time immediately before them. Autobiography followed where biography led. Lord Herbert of Cherbury and Margaret Duchess of Newcastle, as well as less reputable persons, followed the new mode. By the time of the Restoration Pepys and Evelyn were keeping their diaries, and Fox his journal. Just as in poetry the lyric, that is the expression of personal feeling, became more widely practised, more subtle and more sincere, in prose the letter, the journal, and the autobiography formed themselves to meet the new and growing demand for analysis of the feeling and the intimate thoughts and sensations of real men and women. A minor form of literature which had a brief but popular vogue ministered less directly to the same need. The "Character," a brief descriptive essay on a contemporary type—a tobacco seller, an old college butler or the like— was popular because in its own way it matched the newly awakened taste for realism and fact. The drama which in the hands of Ben Jonson had attacked folly and wickedness proper to no place or time, descended to the drawing-rooms of the day, and Congreve occupied himself with the portrayal of the social frauds and foolishness perpetrated by actual living men and women of fasting in contemporary London. Satire ceased to be a mere expression of vague discontent, and became a weapon against opposing men and policies. The new generation of readers were nothing if not critical. They were for testing directly institutions whether they were literary, social, or political. They wanted facts, and they wanted to take a side.

In the distinct and separate realm of poetry a revolution no less remarkable took place. Spenser had been both a poet and a Puritan: he had designed to show by his great poem the training and fashioning of a Puritan English gentleman. But the alliance between poetry and Puritanism which he typified failed to survive his death. The essentially pagan spirit of the Renaissance which caused him no doubts nor difficulties proved too strong for his readers and his followers, and the emancipated artistic enthusiasm in which it worked alienated from secular poetry men with deep and strong religious convictions. Religion and morality and poetry, which in Sidney and Spenser had gone hand in hand, separated from each other. Poems like *Venus and Adonis* or like Shakespeare's sonnets could hardly be squared with the stener temper which persecution began to breed. Even within orthodox Anglicanism poetry and religion began to be deemed no fit company for each other. When George Herbert left off courtier and took orders he burnt his earlier love poetry, and only the persuasion of his friends prevented Donne from following the same course. Pure Poetry became more and more an exotic. All Milton's belongs to his earlier youth; his middle age was occupied with controversy and propaganda in prose; when he returned to poetry in blindness and old age it was "to justify the ways of God to man"—to use poetry, that is, for a spiritual and moral rather than an artistic end.

Though the age was curious and inquiring, though poetry and prose tended more and more to be enlisted in the service of nonartistic enthusiasms and to be made the vehicle of deeper emotions and interests than perhaps a northern people could ever find in art, pure and simple, it was not like the time that followed it, a "prosaic" age. Enthusiasm burned fierce and clear, displaying itself in the passionate polemic of Milton, in the fanaticism of Bunyan and Fox, hardly more than in the gentle, steadfast search for knowledge in Burton and the wide and vigilant curiousness of Bacon. Its eager experimentalism tried the impossible; wrote poems and then gave them a weight of meaning they could not carry, as when Flectcher in *The Purple Island* designed to allegorize all that the physiology of his day knew of the human body, or Donne sought to convey abstruse scientific fact in a lyric. It gave men a passion for pure learning, set Jonson to turn himself from a bricklayer into the best equipped scholar of his day, and Fuller and Camden grubbing among English records and gathering for the first time materials of scientific value for English history. Enthusiasm gave us poetry that was at once full of learning and of imagination, poetry that was harsh and brutal in its roughness and at the same time impassioned. And it set up a school of prose that combined colloquial readiness and fluency, pregnancy and high sentiment with a cumbrous pedantry of learning which was the fruit of its own excess.

The form in which enthusiasm manifested itself most fiercely was as we have seen not favourable to literature. Puritanism drove itself like a wedge into the art of the time, broadening as it went. Had there been no more in it than the moral earnestness and religiousness of Sidney and Spenser, Cavalier would not have differed from Roundhead, and there might have been no civil war; each party was endowed deeply with the religious sense and Charles I was a sincerely pious man. But while Spenser and Sidney held that life as a preparation for eternity must be ordered and strenuous and devout but that are for the hereafter was not incompatible with a frank and full enjoyment of life as it is lived, Puritanism as it developed in the middle classes became a sterner and darker creed. The doctrine of original sin, face to face with the fact that art, like other pleasures, was naturally and readily entered into and enjoyed, forced them to the plain conclusion that art was an evil thing. As early as Shakespeare's youth they had been strong enough to keep the theatres outside London walls; at the time of the Civil War they closed them altogether, and the feud which had lasted for over a generation between them and the dramatists ended in the destruction of the literary drama. In the brief years of their ascendancy they produced no literature, for Milton is much too large to be tied down to their negative creed, and, indeed, in many of his qualities, his love of music and his sensuousness for instance, he is antagonistic to the temper of his day. With the Restoration their earnest and strenuous spirit fled to America. It is noteworthy that it had no literary manifestation there till two centuries after the time of its passage. Hawthorne's novels are the fruit— the one ripe fruit in art—of the Puritan imagination.

If the reader adopts the seventeenth century habit himself and takes stock of what the Elizabethans accomplished in poetry, he will recognize speedily that their work reached various stages of completeness. They perfected the poetic drama and its instrument, blank verse; they perfected, though not in the severer Italian form, the sonnet; they wrote with extraordinary delicacy and finish short lyrics in which a simple and freer manner drawn from the classics took the place of the mediaeval intricacies of the ballad and the rondeau. And in the forms which they failed to bring to perfection they did beautiful and noble work. The splendour of *The Fairy Queen* is in separate passages; as a whole it is over tortuous and slow; its affectations, its sensuousness, the mere difficulty of reading it, makes us feel it a collection of great passages, strung it is true on a large conception, rather than a great work. The Elizabethans, that is, had not discovered the secret of the long poem; the abstract idea of "heroic" epic which was in all their minds had to wait for embodiment till *Paradise Lost*. In a way their treatment of the pastoral or eclogue form was imperfect too. They used it well but not so well as theri models, Vergil and Theocritus; they had not quite mastered the convention on which it is built.

The seventeenth century, taking stock in some such fashion of its artistic possessions, found some things it were vain to try to do. It could add nothing to the accomplishment of the English sonnet, so it hardly tried; with the exception of a few sonnets in the Italian form of Milton, the century can show us nothing in this mode of verse. The literary drama was brought to perfection in the early years of it by the surviving Elizabethans; later decades could add nothing to it but licence, and as we saw, the licences they added hastened its destruction. But in other forms the poets of the new time experiment, poetry which under Elizabeth had been integral and coherent split into different schools. As the period of the Renaissance was also that of the Reformation it was only natural a determined effort should sooner or later be made to use poetry for religious purposes. The earliest English hymn writing, our first devotional verse in the vernacular, belongs to this time, and a Catholic and religious school of lyricism grew and flourished beside the pagan neo-classical writers. From the tumult of experiment three schools disengage themselves, the school of Spenser, the school of Jonson, and the school of Donne.

At the outset of the century Spenser's influence was triumphant and predominant: his was the main stream with which the other poetic influences of the time merely mingled. His popularity is referable to qualities other than those which belonged peculiarly to his talent as a poet. Puritans loved his religious ardour, and in those Puritan households where the stricter conception of the diabolical nature of all poetry had not penetrated, his works were read—standing on a shelf, may be, between the new translation of the Bible and Sylvester's translation of the French poet Du Bartas' work on the creation, that had a large popularity at that time as family reading. Probably the Puritans were as blind to the sensuousness of Spenser's language and imagery as they were (and are) to the same qualities in the Bible itself. *The Fairy Queen* would easily achieve innocuousness amongst those who can find nothing but an allegory of the Church in the "Song of Songs." His followers made their allegory a great deal plainer than he had done his. In his poem called *The Purple Island*, Phineas Fletcher, a Puritan imitator of Spenser in Cambridge, essayed to set forth the struggle of the soul at grip with evil, a battle in which the body—the "Purple Island"—is the field. To a modern reader it is a desolating and at times a mildly amusing book, in which everything from the liver to the seven deadly sins is personified; in which after four books of allegorized contemporary anatomy and physiology, the will (Voletta) engages in a struggle with Satan and conquers by the help of Christ and Kind James! The allegory is clever—too clever—and the author can paint a pleasant picture, but on the whole he was happier in his pastoral work. His brother Giles made a better attempt at the Spenserian manner. His long poem, *Christ's Victory and Death*, shows for all its carefully Protestant tone high qualities of mysticism; across it Spenser and Milton join hands.

It was, however, in pastoral poetry that Spenser's influence found its pleasantest outlet. One might hesitate to advise a reader to embark on either of the Fletchers. There is no reason why any modern should not read and enjoy Browne or Wither, in whose softly flowing verse the sweetness and contentment of the countryside, that "merry England" which was the background of all sectarian and intellectual strife and labour, finds as in a placid stream a calm reflection and picture of itself. The seventeenth century gave birth to many things that only came to maturity in the nineteenth; if you care for that kind of literary study which searches out origins and digs for hints and models of accepted styles, you will find in Browne that which influenced more than any other single thing the early work of Keats. Browne has another claim to immortality; if it be true as is now thought that he was the author of the epitaph on the Countess of Pembroke :

"Underneath this sable hearse
Lies the subject of all verse,
Sidney's sister, Pembroke's mother.
Death, ere thou hast slain another
Fair and learned and good as she,
Time shall throw a dart at thee."

then he achieved the miracle of a quintessential statement of the spirit of the English Renaissance. For the breath of it stirs in these slow quiet moving lines, and its few and simple words implicate the soul of a period.

By the end of the first quarter of the century the influence of Spenser and the school which worked under it had died out. Its place was taken by the twin schools of Jonson and Donne. Jonson's poetic method is something like his dramatic; he formed himself as exactly as possible on classical models. Horace had written satires and elegies, and epistles and complimentary verses, and Jonson quite consciously and deliberately followed where Horace led. He wrote elegies on the great, letters and courtly compliments and love-lyrics to his friends, satires with an air of general censure. But though he was classical, his style was never latinized. In all of them he strove to pour into an ancient form language that was as intense and vigorous and as purely English as the earliest trumpeters of the Renaissance in England could have wished. The result is not entirely successful. He seldom fails to reproduce classic dignity and good sense; on the other hand he seldom succeeds in achieving classic grace and ease. Occasionally, as in his best known lyric, he is perfect and achieves an air of spontaneity little short of marvellous, when we know that his images and even his words in the song are all plagiarized from other men. His expression is always clear and vigorous and his sense good and noble. The native earnestness and sincerity of the man shines through as it does in his dramas and his prose. In an age of fantastic and meaningless eulogy—eulogy so amazing in its unexpectedness and abstruseness that the wonder is not so much that it should have been written as that it could have been thought of—Jonson maintains his personal dignity and his good sense. You feel his compliments are such as the best should be, not necessarily understood and properly valued by the public, but of a discriminating sort that by their very comprehending sincerity would be most warmly appreciated by the people to whom they were addressed. His verses to Shakespeare and his prose commentaries on him too, are models of what self-respecting admiration should be, generous in its praise of excellence, candid in its statement of defects. They are the kind of compliments that Shakespeare himself, if he had grace enough, must have loved to receive.

Very different from his direct and dignified manner is the closely packed style of Donne, who, Milton apart, is the greatest English writer of the century, though his obscurity has kept him out of general reading. No poetry in English, not even Browning, is more difficult to understand. The obscurity of Donne and Browning proceed from such similar causes that they are worth examining together. In both, as in the obscure passages in Shakespeare's later plays, obscurity arises not because the poet says too little but because he attempts to say too much. He huddles a new thought on the one before it, before the first has had time to express itself; he sees things or analyses emotions so swiftly and subtly himself that he forget the slower comprehensions of his readers; he is for analysing things far deeper than the ordinary mind commonly can. His wide and curious knowledge finds terms and likenesses to express his meaning unknown to us; he sees things from a dozen points of view at once and tumbles a hint of each separate vision in a heap out on to the page; his restless intellect finds new and subtler shades of emotion and thought invisible to other pairs of eyes, and cannot, because speech is modelled on the average of our intelligences, find words to express them; he is always trembling on the brink of the inarticulate. All this applies to both Donne and Browning, and the comparison could be pushed further still. Both draw the knowledge which is the main cause of their obscurity from the same source, the bypaths of mediaevalism. Browning's *Sordello* is obscure because he knows too much about mediaeval Italian history; Donne's *Anniversary* because he is too deeply read in mediaeval scholasticism and speculation. Both make themselves more difficult to the reader who is familiar with the poetry of their contemporaries by the disconcerting freshness of their point of view. Seventeenth century love poetry was idyllic and idealist; Donne's is passionate and realistic to the point of cynicism. To read him after reading Browne or Jonson is to have the same shock as reading Browning after Tennyson. Both poets are salutary in the strong and biting antidote they bring to sentimentalism in thought and melodious facility in writing. They are the corrective of lazy thinking and lazy composition.

Elizabethan love poetry was written on a convention which though it was used with manliness and entire sincerity by Sidney did not escape the fate of its kind. Dante's love for Beatrice, Petrarch's for Laura, the gallant and passionate adoration of Sidney for his Stella became the models for a dismal succession of imaginary woes. They war all figments of the mind, perhaps hardly that; they all use the same terms and write in fixed strains, epicurean and sensuous like Ronsard, ideal and intellectualized like Dante, sentimental and adoring like Petrarch. Into this enclosed garden of sentiment and illusion Donne burst passionately and rudely, pulling up the gay-coloured tangled weeds that choked thoughts, planting, as one of his followers said, the seeds of fresh invention. Where his forerunners had been idealist, epicurean, or adoring, he was brutal, cynical and immitigably realist. He could begin a poem, "For God's sake hold your tongue and let me live"; he could be as resolutely free from illusion as Shakespeare when he addressed his Dark Lady—

> "Hope not for mind in women; at their best,
> Sweetness and wit they're but mummy possest."

And where the sonneteers pretended to a sincerity which was none of theirs, he was, like Browning, unaffectedly a dramatic lyrist. "I did best," he said, "when I had least truth for my subject."

His love poetry was written in his turbulent and brilliant youth, and the poetic talent which made it turned in his later years to express itself in hymns and religious poetry. But there is no essential distinction between the two halves of his work. It is all of a piece. The same swift and subtle spirit which analyses experiences of passion, analyses, in his later poetry, those of religion. His devotional poems, though they probe and question, are none the less never sermons, but rather confessions or prayers. His intense individuality, eager always, as his best critic has said, "to find a North-West passage of his own," pressed its curious and sceptical questioning into every corner of love and life and religion, explored unsuspected depths, exploited new discovered paradoxes, and turned its discoveries always into poetry of the closely-packed artificial style which was all its own. Simplicity indeed would have been for him an affectation; his elaborateness is not like that of his followers, constructed painfully in a vicious desire to compass the unexpected, but the natural overflow of an amazingly fertile and ingenious mind. The curiosity, the desire for truth, the search after minute and detailed knowledge of his age is all in his verse. He bears the spirit of his time not less markedly than Bacon does, or Newton, or Descrates.

The work of the followers of Donne and Jonson leads straight to the new school, Jonson's by giving that school a model on which to work, Donne's by producing an era of extravagance and absurdity which made a literary revolution imperative. The school of Donne—the "fantastics" as they have been called (Dr. Johnson called them the metaphysical poets), produced in Herbert and Vaughan, our two noblest writers of religious verse, the flower of a mode of writing which ended in the somewhat exotic religiousness of Crashaw. In the hands of Cowley the use of far-sought and intricate imagery became a trick, and the fantastic school, the soul of sincerity gone out of it, died when he died. To the followers of Jonson we owe that delightful and simple lyric poetry which fills our anthologies, their courtly lyricism receiving a new impulse in the intenser loyalty of troubled times. The most finished of them is perhaps Carew; the best, because of the freshness and varity of his subject-matter and his easy grace, Herrick. At the end of them came Waller and gave to the five-accented rhymed verse (the heroic couplet) that trick of regularity and balance which gave us the classical school.

The prose literature of the seventeenth century is extraordinarily rich and varied, and a study of it would cover a wide field of human knowledge. The new and unsuspected harmonies discovered by the Elizabethans were applied indeed to all the tasks of which prose is capable, from telling stories to setting down the results of speculation which was revolutionizing science and philosophy. For the first time the vernacular and not Latin became the language of scientific research, and though Bacon in his *Novum Organum* adhered to the older mode its disappearance was rapid. English was proving itself too flexible an instrument for conveying ideas to be longer neglected. It was applied too to preaching of a more formal and grandiose kind than the plain and homely Latimer ever dreamed of. The preachers, though their golden-mouthed oratory, which blended in its combination of vigour and cadence the euphuistic and colloquial styles of the Elizabethans, is in itself a glory of English literature, belong by their matter too exclusively to the province of Church history to be dealt with here. The men of science and philosophy, Newton, Hobbes, and Locke, are in a like way outside our province. For the purpose of the literary student the achievement of the seventeenth century can be judged in four separate men or books—in the Bible, in Francis Bacon, and in Burton and Browne.

In a way the Bible, like the preachers, lies outside the domain of literary study in the narrow sense; but its sheer literary magnitude, the abiding significance of it in our subsequent history, social, political, and artistic as well as religious, compel us to turn aside to examine the causes that have produced such great results. The Authorized Version is not, of course, a purely seventeenth century work. Though the scholars who wrote and compiled it had before them all the previous vernacular texts and chose the best readings where they found them or devised new ones in accordance with the original, the basis is undoubtedly the Tudor version of Tindall. It has, none the less, the qualities of the time of its publication. It could hardly have been done earlier; had it been so, it would not have been done half so well. In it English has lost both its roughness and its affectation and retained its strength; the Bible is the supreme example of early English prose style. The reason is not far to seek. Of all recipes for good or noble writing that which enjoins the writer to be careful about the matter and never mind the manner, is the most sure. The translators had the handling of matter of the gravest dignity and momentousness, and their sense of reverence kept them right in their treatment of it. They cared passionately for the truth; they were virtually anonymous and not ambitious of originality or literary fame; they had no desire to stand between the book and its readers. It followed that they cultivated that naked plainness and spareness which makes their work supreme. The Authorized Version is the last and greatest of those English translations which were the fruit of Renaissance scholarship and pioneering. It is the first and greatest piece of English prose.

Its influence is one of those things on which it is profitless to comment or enlarge simply because they are an understood part of every man's experience. In its own time it helped to weld England, for where before one Bible was read at home and another in churches, all now read the new version. Its supremacy was instantaneous and unchallenged, and it quickly coloured speech and literature; it could produce a Bunyan in the century of its birth. To it belongs the native dignity and eloquence of peasant speech. It runs like a golden thread through all our writing subsequent to its coming; men so diverse as Huxley and Carlyle have paid their tribute to its power; Ruskin counted it the one essential part of its education. It will be a bad day for the mere quality of our language when it ceases to be read.

At the time the translators were sitting, Francis Bacon was at the height of his fame. By profession a lawyer—time-serving and over-compliant to wealth and influence—he gives singularly little evidence of it in the style of his books. Lawyers, from the necessity they are under of exerting persuasion, of planting an unfamiliar argument in the minds of hearers of whose favour they are doubtful, but whose sympathy they must gain, are usually of purpose diffuse. They cultivate the gift, possessed by Edmund Burke above all other English authors, of putting the same thing freshly and in different forms a great many times in succession. They value copiousness and fertility of illustration. Nothing could be more unlike this normal legal manner than the style of Bacon. "No man," says Ben Jonson, speaking in one of those vivid little notes of his, of his oratorical method, "no man ever coughed or turned aside from him without loss." He is a master of the aphoristic style. He compresses his wisdom into the quintessential form of an epigram; so complete and concentrated is his form of statement, so shortly is everything put, that the mere transition from one thought to another gives his prose a curious air of disjointedness as if he flitted arbitrarily from one thing to another, and jotted down anything that came into his head. His writing has clarity and lucidity, it abounds in terseness of expression and in exact and discriminating phraseology, and in the minor arts of composition—in the use of quotations for instance—it can be extraordinarily felicitous. But it lacks spaciousness and ease and rhythm; it makes too inexorable a demand on the attention, and the harassed reader soon finds himself longing for those breathing spaces which consideration or perhaps looseness of thought has implanted in the prose of other writers.

His *Essays*, the work by which he is best known, were in their origin merely jottings gradually cohered and enlarged into the series we know. In them he had the advantage of a subject which he had studied closely through life. He counted himself a master in the art of managing men, and "Human Nature and how to manage it" would be a good title for his book. Men are studied in the spirit of Machiavelli, whose philosophy of government appealed so powerfully to the Elizabethan mind. Taken together the essays which deal with public matters are in effect a kind of manual for statesmen and princes, instructing them how to acquire power and how to keep it, deliberating how far they many go safely in the direction of self-interest, and to what degree the principle of self-interest must be subordinated to the wider interests of the people who are ruled. Democracy, which in England was to make its splendid beginnings in the seventeenth century, finds little to foretell it in the works of Bacon. Though he never advocates cruelty or oppression and is wise enough to see that no statesman can entirely set aside moral considerations, his ethical tone is hardly elevating; the moral obliquity of his public life is to a certain extent explained, in all but its grosser elements, in his published writings. The essays, of course, contain much more than this; the spirit of curious and restless enquiry which animated Bacon finds expression in those on "Health," or "Gardens" and "Plantations" and others of the kind; and a deeper vein of earnestness runs through some of them—those for instance on "Friendship," or "Truth" and on "Death."

The *Essays* sum up in a condensed form the intellectual interests which find larger treatment in his other works. His *Henry VII.*, the first piece of scientific history in the English language (indeed in the modern world) is concerned with a king whose practice was the outcome of a political theory identical with Bacon's own. The *Advancement of Learning* is a brilliant popular exposition of the cause of scientific enquiry and of the inductive or investigatory method of research. The *New Atlantis* is the picture of an ideal community whose common purpose is scientific investigation. Bacon's name is not upon the roll of those who have enlarged by brilliant conjectures or discoveries the store of human knowledge; his own investigations so far as they are recorded are all of a trivial nature. The truth about him is that he was a brilliantly clever populariser of the cause of science, a kind of seventeenth century Huxley, concerned rather to lay down large general principles for the guidance of the work of others, than to be a serious worker himself. The superstition of later times, acting on and refracting his amazing intellectual gifts, has raised him to a godlike eminence which is by right none of his; it has even credited him with the authorship of Shakespeare, and in its wilder moments with the composition of áll that is of supreme worth in Elizabethan literature. It is not necessary to take these delusions seriously. The ignorance of mediævalism was in the habit of crediting Vergil with the construction of the Roman aqueducts and temples whose ruins are scattered over Europe. The modern Baconians reach much the same intellectual level.

A similar enthusiasm for knowledge and at any rate a pretence to science belong to the author of the *Anatomy of Melancholy*, Robert Burton. His one book is surely the most amazing in English prose. Its professed object was simple and comprehensive; it was to analyze human melancholy, to describe its effects, and prescribe for its removal. But as his task grew, melancholy came to mean to Burton all the ills that flesh is heir to. He tracked it in obscure and unsuspected forms;

drew illustrations from a range of authors so much wider than the compass of the reading of even the most learned since, that he is generally credited with the invention of a large part of his quotations. Ancients and moderns, poets and prose writers, schoolmen and dramatists are all drawn upon for the copious store of his examples; they are always cited with an air of quietly humorous shrewdness in the comments and enclosed in a prose that is straightforward, simple and vigorous, and can on occasion command both rhythm and beauty of phrase. It is a mistake to regard Burton from the point of view (due largely to Charles Lamb) of tolerant or loving delight in quaintness for quaintness' sake. His book is anything but scientific in form, but it is far from being the work of a recluse or a fool. Behind his lack of system, he takes a broad and psychologically an essentially just view of human ills, and modern medicine has gone far in its admiration of what is at bottom a most comprehensive and subtle treatise in diagnosis.

A writer of a very different quality is Sir Thomas Browne. Of all the men of his time, he is the only one of whom one can say for certain that he held the manner of saying a thing more important than the thing said. He is our first deliberate and conscious stylist, the forerunner of Charles Lamb, of Stevenson (whose *Virginibus Puerisque* is modelled on his method of treatment) and of the stylistic school of our own day. His eloquence is too studied to rise to the greatest heights, and his speculation, though curious and discursive, never really results in deep thinking. He is content to embroider his pattern out of the stray fancies of an imaginative nature. His best known work, the *Religio Medici*, is a random confession of belief and thoughts, full of the inconsequent speculations of a man with some knowledge of science but not deeply or earnestly interested about it, content rather to follow the wayward imaginations of a mind naturally gifted with a certain poetic quality, than to engage in serious intellectual exercise. Such work could never maintain its hold on taste if it were not carefully finished and constructed with elaborate care. Browne, if he was not a great writer, was a literary artist of a high quality. He exploits a quaint and lovable egoism with extraordinary skill; and though his delicately figured and latinized sentences commonly sound platitudinous and trivial when they are translated into rough Saxon prose, as they stand they are rich and melodious enough.

In a century of surpassing richness in prose and poetry, one author stands by himself. John Milton refuses to be classed with any of the schools. Though Dryden tells us Milton confessed to him that Spenser was his "original," he has no connection—other than a general similarity of purpose, moral and religious—with Spenser's followers. To the fantastics he paid in his youth the doubtful compliment of one or two half-contemptuous imitations and never touched them again. He had no turn for the love lyrics or the courtliness of the school of Jonson. In everything he did he was himself and his own master; he devised his own subjects and wrote his own style. He stands alone and must be judged alone.

No author, however, can ever escape from the influences of his time, and, just as much as his lesser contemporaries, Milton has his place in literary history and derives from the great original impulse which set in motion all the enterprises of the century. He is the last and greatest figure in the English Renaissance. The new passion for art and letters which in its earnest fumbling beginnings gave us the prose of cheek and Ascham and the poetry of Surrey and Sackville, comes to a full and splendid and perfect end in his work. In it the Renaissance and the Reformation, imperfectly fused by Sidney and Spenser, blend in their just proportions. The transplantation into English of classical forms which had been the aim of Sidney and the endeavour of Jonson he finally accomplished; in his work the dream of all the poets of the Renaissance—the heroic poem—finds its fulfilment. There was no poet of the time but wanted to do for his country what Vergil had planned to do for Rome, to sing its origins, and to celebrate its morality and its citizenship in the epic form. Spenser had tried it in *The Fairy Queen* and failed splendidly. Where he failed, Milton succeeded, though his poem is not on the origins of England but on the ultimate subject of the origins of mankind. We know from his note-books that he turned over in his mind a national subject and that the Arthurian legend for a while appealed to him. But to Milton's earnest temper nothing that was not true was a fit subject for poetry. It was inevitable he should lay it aside. The Arthurian story he knew to be a myth and a myth was a lie; the story of the Fall, on the other hand he accepted in common with his time for literal fact. It is to be noted as characteristic of his confident and assured egotism that he accepted no less sincerely and literally the imaginative structure which he himself reared on it. However that may be, the solid fact about him is that in this "adventurous song" with its pursuit of

> "Things unattempted yet in prose or rhyme,"

he succeeded in his attempt, that alone among the moderns he contrived to write an epic which stands on the same eminence as the ancient writings of the kind, and that he found time in a life, which hardly extended to old age as we know it, to write, besides noble lyrics and a series of fiercely argumentative prose treatises, two other masterpieces in the grand style, a tragedy modelled on the Greeks and a second epic on the "compact" style of the book of Job. No English poet can compare with him in majesty or completeness.

An adequate study of his achievement is impossible within the limits of the few pages that are all a book like this can spare to a single author. Readers who desire it will find it in the work of his two best critics, Mark Pattison and Sir Walter Raleigh. All that can be done here is to call attention to some of his most striking qualities. Foremost, of course, is the temper of the man. From the beginning he was sure of himself and sure of his mission; he had his purpose plain and clear. There is no mental development, hardly, visible in his work, only training, undertaken anxiously and prayerfully and with a clearly conceived end. He designed to write a masterpiece and he would not start till he was ready. The first twenty years of his life were spent in assiduous reading; for twenty more he was immersed in the dust and toil of political conflict, using his pen and his extraordinary equipment of learning and eloquence to defend the cause of liberty, civil and religious, and to attack its enemies; not till he was past middle age had he reached the leisure and the preparedness necessary to accomplish his self-imposed work. But all the time, as we know, he had it in his mind. In *Lycidas*, written in his Cambridge days, he apologizes to his readers for plucking the fruit of his poetry before it is ripe. In passage after passage in his prose works he begs for his reader's patience for a little while longer till his preparation be complete. When the time came at last for beginning he was in no doubt; in his very opening lines he intends, he says, to soar no "middle flight." This self-assured unrelenting certainty of his, carried into his prose essays in argument, produces sometimes strange results. One is peculiarly interesting to us now in view of current controversy. He was unhappily married, and because he was unhappy the law of divorce must be changed. A modern—George Eliot for instance—would have pleaded the artistic temperament and been content to remain outside the law. Milton always argued from himself to mankind at large.

In everything he did, he put forth all his strength. Each of his poems, long or short, is by itself a perfect whole, wrought complete. The reader always must feel that the planning of each is the work of conscious, deliberate, and selecting art. Milton never digresses; he never violates harmony of sound or sense; his poems have all their regular movement from quiet beginning through a rising and breaking wave of passion and splendour to quiet close. His art is nowhere better seen than in his endings.

Is it *Lycidas*? After the thunder of approaching vengeance on the hireling shepherds of the Church, comes sunset and quiet :

> " And now the sun had stretch'd out all the hills,
> And now was dropt into the western bay;
> At last he rose, and twitched his mantle blue;
> To-morrow to fresh woods and pastures new."

Is it *Paradise Lost*? After the agonies of expulsion and the flaming sword—

> " Some natural tears they drop'd, but wip'd them
> soon;
> The world was all before them where to choose
> Their place of rest, and Providence their guide;
> They hand in hand with wandering steps and
> slow,
> Through Eden took their solitary way."

Is it finally *Samson Agonistes* ?

> " His servants he with new acquist,
> Of true experience from this great event,
> With peace and consolation hath dismist,
> And calm of mind all passion spent."

"Calm of mind, all passion spent," it is the essence of Milton's art.

He worked in large ideas and painted splendid canvases; it was necessary for him to invent a style which should be capable of sustained and lofty dignity, which should be ornate enough to maintain the interest of the reader and charm him and at the same time not so ornate as to give an air of meretricious decoration to what was largely and simply conceived. Particularly it was necessary for him to avoid those incursions of vulgar associations which words carelessly used will bring in their train. He succeeded brilliantly in this difficult task. The unit of the Miltonic style is not the phrase but the word, each word fastidiously chosen, commonly with some air of an original and lost meaning about it, and all set in a verse in which he contrived by an artful variation of pause and stress to give the variety which other writers had from rhyme. In this as in his structure he accomplished what the Renaissance had only dreamed. Though he had imitators (the poetic diction of the age following is modelled on him) he had no followers. No one has been big enough to find his secret since.

The Age of Good Sense

The student of literature, when he passes in his reading from the age of Shakespeare and Milton to that of Dryden and Pope, will be conscious of certain sharply defined differences between the temper and styles of the writers of the two periods. If besides being a student of literature he is also (for this is a different thing) a student of literary criticism he will find that these differences have led to the affixing of certain labels—that the school to which writers of the former period belong is called "Romantic" to themselves. What is he to understand by these two labels; what are the characteristics of "Classicism" and how far is it opposite to and conflicting with "Romanticism" ? The question is difficult because the names are used vaguely and they do not adequately cover everything that is commonly put under them. It would be difficult, for instance, to find anything in Ben Jonson which proclaims him as belonging to a different school from Dryden, and perhaps the same could be said in the second and self-styled period of Romanticism of the work of Crabbe. But in the main the differences are real and easily visible, even though they hardly convince us that the names chosen are the happiest that could be found by way of description.

This period of Dryden and Pope on which we are now entering sometimes styled itself the Augustan Age of English poetry. It grounded its claim to classicism on a fancied resemblance to the Roman poets of the golden age of Latin poetry, the reign of the Emperor Augustus. Its authors saw themselves each as a second Vergil, a second Ovid, most of all a second Horace, and they believed that their relation to the big world, their assured position in society, heightened the resemblances. They endeavoured to form heir poetry on the lines laid down in the critical writing of the original Augustan age as elaborated and interpreted in Renaissance criticism. It was tacitly assumed—some of them openly asserted it—that the kinds, modes of treatment and all the minor details of literature, figures of speech, use of epithets and the rest, had been settled by the ancients once and for all. What the Greeks began the critics and authors of the time of Augustus had settled in its completed form, and the scholars of the Renaissance had only interpreted their findings for modern use. There was the tragedy, which had certain proper parts and a certain fixed order of treatment laid down for it; there was the heroic poem, which had a story or "fable," which must be treated in a certain fixed manner, and so on. The authors of the "Classic" period so christened themselves because they observed these rules. And they fancied that they had the temper of the Augustan time—the temper displayed in the works of Horace more than in those of any one else—its urbanity, its love of good sense and moderation, its instinctive distrust of emotion, and its invincible good breeding. If you had asked them to state as simply and broadly as possible their purpose they would have said it was to follow nature, and if you had enquired what they meant by nature it would turn out that they thought of it mainly as the opposite of art and the negation of what was fantastic, tortured, or far sought in thinking or writing. The later "Romantic" Revival, when it called itself a return to nature, was only claiming the intention which the classical school itself had proclaimed as its main endeavour. The explanation of that paradox we shall see presently; in the meantime it is worth looking at some of the characteristics of classicism as they appear in the work of the "Classic" authors.

In the first place the "Classic" writers aimed at simplicity of style, at a normal standard of writing. They were intolerant of individual eccentricities; they endeavoured, and with success, to infuse into English letters something of the academic spirit that was already controlling their fellow-craftsmen in France. For this end amongst others they and the men of science founded the Royal Society, an academic committee which has been restricted since to the physical and natural sciences and been supplemented by similar bodies representing literature and learning only in our own day. Clearness, plainness, conversational ease and directness were the aims the society set before its members where their writing was concerned. "The Royal Society," wrote the Bishop of Rochester, its first historian, "have exacted from all their members a close, naked, natural way of speaking; positive expressions, clear sense, a native easiness, bringing all things as near the mathematical plainness as they can; and preferring the language of artisans, countrymen, and merchants before that of wits and scholars." Artisans, countrymen, and merchants—the ideal had been already accepted in France, Malesherbes striving to use no word that was not in the vocabulary of the day labourers of Paris, Molière making his washerwoman first critic of his comedies. It meant for England the disuse of the turgidities and involutions which had marked the prose of the preachers and moralists of the times of James and Charles I.; scholars and men of letters were arising who would have taken John Bunyan, the unlettered tinker of Bedord, for their model rather than the learned physician Sir Thomas Browne.

But genius like Bunyan's apart, there is nothing in the world more difficult than to write with the easy and forthright simplicity of talk, as any one may see who tries for himself—or even compares the letter-writing with the conversation of his friends. So that this desire of simplicity, of clarity, of lucidity led at once to a more deliberate art. Dryden and Swift and Addison were assiduous in their labour with the file; they excel all their predecessors in polish as much as the writers of the first Augustan age excelled theirs in the same quality. Not that it was all the result of deliberate art; in a way it was in the air, and quite unlearned people—journalists and pamphleteers and the like who wrote unconsciously and hurriedly to buy their supper—partook of it as well as leisured people and conscious artists. Defoe is as plain and easy and polished as Swift, yet it is certain his amazing activity and productiveness never permitted him to look back over a sentence he had written. Something had happened, that is, to the English language. The assimilation of latinisms and the revival of obsolete terms of speech had ceased; it had become finally a more or less fixed form, shedding so much of its imports as it had failed to make part of itself and acquiring a grammatical and syntactical fixity which it had not possessed in Elizabethan times. When Shakespeare wrote

"What cares these roarers for the name of king."

he was using, as students of his language never tire of pointing out to us, a perfectly correct local grammatical form. Fifty years after that line was written, at the Restoration, local forms had dropped out of written English. We had acquired a normal standard of language, and either genius or labour was polishing it for literary uses.

What they did for prose these "Classic" writers did even more exactly—and less happily—for verse. Fashions often become exaggerated before their disappearance, and the decadence of Elizabethan romanticism had produced poetry the wildness and extravagance of whose images was well-nigh unbounded. The passion for intricate and far-sought metaphor which had possessed Donne was accompanied in his work and even more in that of his followers with a passion for what was elusive and recondite in thought and emotion and with an increasing habit of rudeness and wilful difficultness in language and versification. Against these ultimate licences of a great artistic period, the classical writers invoked the qualities of smoothness and lucidity, in the same way, so they fancied, as Vergil might have invoked them against Lucretius. In the treatment of thought and feeling they wanted clearness, they wanted ideas which the mass of men would readily apprehend and assent to, and they wanted not hints or half-spoken suggestions but complete statement. In the place of the logical subtleties which Donne and his school had sought in the scholastic writers of the Middle Ages, they brought back the typically Renaissance study of rhetoric; the characteristic of all the poetry of the period is that it has a rhetorical quality. It is never intimate and never profound, but it has point and wit, and it appeals with confidence to the balanced judgment which men who distrust emotion and have no patience with subtleties intellectual, emotional, or merely verbal, have in common. Alongside of this lucidity, this air of complete statement in substance, they strove for and achieved smoothness in form. To the poet Waller, the immediate predecessor of Dryden, the classical writers themselves ascribed the honour of the innovation. In fact Waller was only carrying out the ideals counselled and followed by Ben Jonson. It was in the school of Waller and Dryden and not in that of the minor writers who called themselves his followers that he came to his own.

What then are the main differences between classicism of the best period—the classicism whose characteristics we have been describing—and the Romanticism which came before and after ? In the first place we must put the quality we have described as that of complete statement. Classical poetry is, so to speak, "all there." Its meaning is all of it on the surface; it conveys nothing but what it says, and what it says, it says completely. It is always vigorous and direct, often pointed and aphoristic, never merely suggestive, never given to half statement, and never obscure. You feel that as an instrument of expression it is sharp and polished and shining; it is always bright and defined in detail. The Great Romantics go to work in other ways. Their poetry is a thing of half lights and half spoken suggestions, of hints that imagination will piece together, of words that are charged with an added meaning of sound over sense, a thing that stirs the vague and impalpable restlessness of memory or terror or desire that lies down beneath in the minds of men. It rouses what a philosopher has called the "Transcendental feeling," the solemn sense of the immediate presence of "that which was and is and ever shall be," to induce which is the property of the highest poetry. You will find nothing in classical poetry so poignant or highly wrought as Webster's

> "Cover her face; mine eyes dazzle; she died
> young."

and the answer,

> "I think not so : her infelicity
> Seemed to have years too many."

or so subtle in its suggestion, sense echoing back to primeval terrors and despairs, as this from *Macbeth* :

> "Stones have been known to move and trees to
> speak;
> Augurs and understood relations have
> By magot-pies, and choughs, and rooks brought
> forth
> The secret'st man of blood."

or so intoxicating to the imagination and the senses as an ode of Keats or a sonnet by Rossetti. But you will find eloquent and pointed statements of thoughts and feelings that are common to most of us—the expression of ordinary human nature—

> "What oft was thought but ne'er so well exprest,"

"Wit and fine writing" consisting, as Addison put it in a review of Pope's first published poem, not so much "in advancing things that are new, as in giving things that are known an agreeable turn."

Though in this largest sense the "classic" writers eschewed the vagueness of romanticism, in another and more restricted way they cultivated it. They were not realists as all good romanticists have to be. They had no love for oddities or idiosyncrasies or exceptions. They loved uniformity, they had no use for truth in detail. They liked the broad generalized, descriptive style of Milton, for instance, better than the closely packed style of Shakespeare, which gets its effects from a series of minute observations huddled one after the other and giving the reader, so to speak, the materials for his own impression, rather than rendering, as does Milton, the expression itself.

Every literary discovery hardens ultimately into a convention; it has its day and then its work is done, and it has to be destroyed so that the ascending spirit of humanity can find a better means of self-expression. Out of the writing which aimed at simplicity and truth to nature grew. "Poetic Diction," a special treasury of words and phrases deemed suitable for poetry, providing poets with a common stock of imagery, removing from them the necessity of seeing life and nature each one for himself. The poetry which Dryden and Pope wrought out of their mental vigour, their followers wrote to pattern. Poetry became reduced, as it never was before and has never been since, to a formula. The Elizabethan sonneteers, as we saw, used a vocabulary and phraseology in common with their fellows in Italy and France, and none the less produced fine poetry. But they used it to express things they really felt. The truth is it is not the fact of a poetic diction which matters so much as its quality--whether it squares with sincerity, whether it is capable of expressing powerfully and directly one's deepest feelings. The history of literature can show poetic dictions—special vocabularies and forms for poetry—that have these qualities; the diction, for instance, of the Greek choruses, or of the Scottish poets who followed Chaucer, or of the troubadours. Threat of the classic writers of an Augustan age was not of such a kind. Words clothe thought; poetic diction had the artifice of the crinoline; it would stand by itself. The Romantics in their return to nature had necessarily to abolish it.

But when all is said in criticism the poetry of the earlier half of the eighteenth century excels all other English poetry in two respects. Two qualities belong to it by virtue of the meter in which it is most of it written--rapidity and antithesis. Its antithesis made it an incomparable vehicle for satire, its rapidity for narrative. Outside its limits we have hardly any even passable satirical verse; within them there are half-a-dozen works of the highest excellence in this kind. And if we except Chaucer, there is no one else in the whole range of English poetry who have the narrative gift so completely as the classic poets. Bentleys will always exist who will assure us with civility that Pope's *Homer*, though "very pretty," bears little relation to the Greek, and that Dryden's *Vergil*, though vigorous and virile, is a poor representation of its original. The truth remains that for a reader who knows no ancient languages either of those translations will probably give a better idea of their originals than any other rendering in English that we possess. The foundation of their method has been vindicated in the best modern translations from the Greek.

The term "eighteenth century" in the vocabulary of the literary historian is commonly as vaguely used as the term Elizabethan. It borrows as much as forty years from the seventeenth and gives away ten to the nineteenth. The whole of the work of Dryden, whom we must count as the first of the "classic" school, was accomplished before chronologically it had begun. As a man and as an author he was very intimately related to his changing times; he adapted himself to them with a versatility as remarkable as that of the Vicar of Bray, and, it may be added, as simple-minded. He mourned in verse the death of Cromwell and the death of his successor, successively defended the theological positions of the Church of England and the Church of Rome, changed his religion and became Poet Laureate to James II., and acquiesced with perfect equanimity in the Revolution which brought in his successor. This instability of conviction, though it gave a handle to his opponents in controversy, does not appear to have caused any serious scandal or disgust among his contemporaries, and it has certainly had little effect on the judgment of later times. It has raised none of the reproaches which have been cast at the suspected apostasy of Wordsworth. Dryden had little interest in political or religious questions; his instinct, one must conceive, was to conform to the prevailing mode and to trouble himself no further about the matter. Defoe told the truth about him when he wrote that "Dryden might have been told his fate that, having his extraordinary genius slung and pitched upon a swivel, it would certainly turn round as fast as the times, and instruct him how to write elegies to Oliver Cromwell and King Charles the Second with all the coherence imaginable; how to write *Relgio Laici* and the *Hind and the Panther* and yet be the same man, every day to change his principle, change his religion, change his coat, change his master, and yet never change his nature." He never changed his nature, he was as free from cynicism as a barrister who represents successively opposing parties in suits or politics; and when he wrote polemics in prose or verse he lent his talents as a barrister lends his for a fee. His one intellectual interest was in his art, and it is in his comments on his art—the essays and prefaces in the composition of which he amused the leisure left in the busy life of a dramatist and a poet of officialdom—that his most charming and delicate work is to be found. In a way they begin modern English prose; earlier writing furnishes no equal to their colloquial ease and the grace of their expression. And they contain some of the most acute criticism in our language—"classical" in its tone (*i.e.*, with a preference for conformity) but with its respect for order and tradition always tempered by good sense and wit, and informed and guided throughout by a taste whose catholicity and sureness was unmatched in the England of his time. The preface to his *Fables* contains some excellent notes on Chaucer. They may be read as a sample of the breadth and perspicuity of his critical perceptions.

His chief poetical works were most of them occasional—designed either to celebrate some remarkable event or to take a side and interpret a policy in the conflict, political or religious, of the time. *Absalom and Achitophel* and *The Medal* were levelled at the Shaftes-bury-Monmouth intrigues in the closing years of Charles II. *Religio Laici* celebrated the excellence of the Church of England in its character of *via media* between the opposite extravagances of Papacy and Presbyterianism. *The Hind and the Panther* found this perfection spotted. The Church of England has become the Panther, whose coat is a varied pattern of heresy and truth beside the spotless purity of the Hind, the Church of Rome. *Astrea Reddux* welcomed the returning Charles; *Annus Mirabilis* commemorated a year of fire and victories. Besides these he wrote many dramas in verse a number of translations, and some shorter poems, of which the odes are the most remarkable.

His qualities as a poet fitted very exactly the work he set himself to do. His work is always plain and easily understood; he had a fine faculty for narration, and the vigorous rapidity and point of his style enabled him to sketch a character or sum up a dialectical position very surely and effectively. His writing has a kind of spare and masculine force about it. It is this vigour and the impression which he gives of intellectual strength and of a logical grasp of his subject, that beyond question has kept alive work which, if ever poetry was, was ephemeral in its origin. The careers of the unscrupulous Caroline peers would have been closed for us were they not visible in the reflected light of his denunciation of them. Though Buckingham is forgotten and Shaftesbury's name swallowed up in that of his more philanthropic descendant, we can read of Achitophel and Zimri still, and feel something of the strength and heat which he caught from a fiercely fought conflict and transmitted with his own gravity and purposefulness into verse. The Thirty-nine Articles are not a proper subject for poetry, but the sustained and serious allegory which Dryden weaves round theological discussion preserves his treatment of them from the fate of the controversialists who opposed him. His work has wit and vitality enough to keep it sweet.

Strength and wit enter in different proportions into the work of his successor. Alexander Pope—a poet whom admirers in his own age held to be the greatest in our language. No one would think of making such a claim now, but the detraction which he suffered at the hands of Wordsworth and the Romantics, ought not to make us forget that Pope, though not our greatest, not even perhaps a great, poet is incomparably our most brilliant versifier. Dryden's strength turns in his work into something more fragile and delicate, polished with infinite care like lacquer, and wrought like filigree work to the last point of conscious and perfected art. He was not a great thinker; the thoughts which he embodies in his philosophical poems—the *Essay on Man* and the rest, are almost ludicrously out of proportion to the solemnity of the titles which introduce them, nor does he except very rarely get beyond the conceptions common to the average man when he attempts introspection or meditates on his own destiny. The reader in search of philosophy will find little to stimulate him and in the facile deism of the time probably something to smile at. Pope has no message to us now. But he will find views current in his time or borrowed from other authors put with perfect felicity and wit, and he will recognize the justice of Addison's comment that Pope's wit and fine writing consist "not so much in advancing things that are new, as in giving things that are known an agreeable turn." And he will not fall into the error of dubbing the author a minor poet because he is neither subtle nor imaginative nor profound. A great poet would not have written like Pope—one must grant it; but a minor poet could not.

It is characteristic of Pope's type of mind and kind of art that there is no development visible in his work. Other poets, Shakespeare, for instance, and Keats, have written work of the highest quality when they were young, but they have had crudenesses to shed—things to get rid of as their strength and perceptions grew. But Pope, like Minerva, was full grown and full armed from the beginning. If we did not know that his *Essay on Criticism* was his first poem it would be impossible to place it in the canon of his work; it might come in anywhere and so might everything else that he wrote. From the beginning his craftsmanship was perfect; from the beginning he took his subject-matter from others as he found it and worked it up into aphorism and epigram till each line shone like a cut jewel and the essential commonplaceness and poverty of his material was obscured by the glitter the craftsmanship lent to it. Subject apart, however, he was quite sure of his medium from the beginning; it was not long before he found the way to use it to most brilliant purpose. *The Rape of the Lock* and the satirical poems come later in his career.

As a satirist Pope, though he did not hit so hard as Dryden, struck more deftly and probed deeper. He wielded a rapier where the other used a broadsword, and though both used their weapons with the highest skill and the metaphor must not be imagined to impute clumsiness to Dryden, the rapier made the cleaner cut. Both employed a method in satire which their successors (a poor set) in England have not been intelligent enough to use. They allow every possible good point to the object of their attack. They appear to deal him an even and regretful justice. His good points, they put it in effect, being so many, how much blacker and more deplorable his meannesses and faults ! They do not do this out of charity; there was very little of the milk of human kindness in Pope. Deformity in his case, as in so many in truth and fiction, seemed to bring envy, hatred, malice and all uncharitableness in its train. The method is employed simply because it gives the maximum satirical effect. That is why Pope's epistle to Arbuthnot, with its characterization of Addison, is the most damning piece of invective in our language.

The Rape of the Lock is an exquisite piece of workmanship, breathing the very spirit of the time. You can fancy it like some clock made by one of the Louis XIV, craftsmen, encrusted with a heap of ormulu mock-heroics and impertinences and set perfectly to the time of day. From no other poem could you gather so fully and perfectly the temper of the society in which our "classic" poetry was brought to perfection, its elegant assiduity in trifles, its brilliant artifice, its paint and powder and patches and high-heeled shoes, its measured strutting walk in life as well as in verse. *The Rape of the Lock* is a mock-heroic poem; that is to say it applies the form and treatment which the "classic" critics of the seventeenth century had laid down as belonging to the "heroic" or "epic" style to a trifling circumstance—the loss by a young lady of fashion of a lock of hair. And it is the one instance in which this "recipe" for a heroic poem which the French critics handed on to Dryden, and Dryden left to his descendants, has been used well-enough to keep the work done with it in memory. In a way it condemns the poetical theory of the time; when forms are fixed, new writing is less likely to be creative and more likely to exhaust itself in the ingenious but trifling exercises of parody and burlesque. *The Rape of the Lock* is brilliant but it is only play.

The accepted theory which assumed that the forms of poetry had been settled in the past and existed to be applied, though it concerned itself mainly with the ancient writers, included also two moderns in its scope. You were orthodox if you wrote tragedy and epic as Horace told you and satire as he had shown you; you were also orthodox if you wrote in the styles of Spenser or Milton. Spenser, though his predecessors were counted barbaric and his followers tortured and obscure, never fell out of admiration; indeed in every age of English poetry after him the greatest poet in it is always to be found copying him or expressing their love for him—Milton declaring to Dryden that Spenser was his "original," Pope reading and praising him, Keats writing his earliest work in close imitation. His characteristic style and stanza were recognized by the classic school as a distinct "kind" of poetry which might be used where the theme fitted instead of the heroic manner, and Spenserian imitations abound. Sometimes they are serious; sometimes, like Shenstone's *Schoolmistress*, they are mocking and another illustration of the dangerous case with which a conscious and sustained effort to write in a fixed and acquired style runs to seed in burlesque. Milton's fame never passed through the period of obscurity that sometimes has been imagined for him. He had the discerning admiration of Dryden and others before his death. But to Addison belongs the credit of introducing him to the writers of this time; his papers in the *Spectator* on *Paradise Lost*, with their eulogy of its author's sublimity, spurred the interest of the poets among his readers. From Milton the eighteenth century got the chief and most ponderous part of its poetic diction, high-sounding periphrases and borrowings from Latin used without the gravity and sincerity and fullness of thought of the master who brought them in. When they wrote blank verse, the classic poets wrote it in the Milton manner.

The use of these two styles may be studied in the writings of one man, James Thomson. For besides acquiring a kind of anonymous immortality with patriots as the author of "Rule, Britannia," Thomson wrote two poems respectively in the Spenserian and the Miltonic manner, the former *The Castle of Indolence*, the latter *The Seasons*. The Spenserian manner is caught very effectively, but the adoption of the style of *Paradise Lost*, with its allusiveness, circumlocution and weight, removes any freshness the *Seasons* might have had, had the circumstances in them been put down as they were observed. As it is, hardly anything is directly named; birds are always the "feathered tribe" and everything else has a similar polite generality for its title. Thomson was a simple-minded man, with a faculty for watching and enjoying nature which belonged to few in his sophisticated age; it is unfortunate he should have spent his working hours in rendering the fruit of country rambles freshly observed into a cold and stilted diction. It suited the eighteenth century reader well, for not understanding nature herself he was naturally obliged to read her in translations.

The chief merits of "classic" poetry—its clearness, its vigour, its direct statement—are such as belong theoretically rather to prose than to poetry. In fact, it was in prose that the most vigorous intellect of the time found itself. We have seen how Dryden, reversing the habit of other poets, succeeded in expressing his personality not in poetry which was his vocation, but in prose which was the amusement of his leisure hours. Spenser had put his politics into prose and his ideals into verse; Dryden wrote his politics—to order— in verse, and in prose set down the thoughts and fancies which were the deepest part of him because they were about his art. The metaphor of parentage, though honoured by use, fits badly on to literary history; none the less the tradition which describes him as the father of modern English prose is very near the truth. He puts into practice for the first time the ideals, described in the first chapter of this book, which were set up by the scholars who let into English the light of the Renaissance. With the exception of the dialogue on Dramatic Poesy, his work is almost all of it occasional, the fruit of the mood of a moment, and written rather in the form of a *causerie*, a kind of informal talk, than of a considered essay. And it is all couched in clear, flowing, rather loosely jointed English, carefully avoiding rhetoric and eloquence and striving always to reproduce the ease and flow of cultured conversation, rather than the tighter, more closely knit style of consciously "literary" prose. His methods were the methods of the four great prose-writers who followed him—Defoe, Addison, Steele, and Swift.

Of these Defoe was the eldest and in some ways the most remarkable. He has been called the earliest professional author in our language, and if that is not strictly true, he is at any rate the earliest literary journalist. His output of work was enormous; he wrote on any and every subject; there was no event whether in politics or letters or discovery but he was not ready with something pat on it before the public interest faded. It followed that at a time when imprisonment, mutilation, and the pillory took the place of our modern libel actions he had an adventurous career. In politics he followed the Whig cause and served the Government with his pen, notably by his writings in support of the union with Scotland, in which he won over the Scots by his description of the commercial advantage which would follow the abolition of the border. This line of argument, taken at a time when the governing of political tendencies by commercial interests was by no means the accepted commonplace it is now, proves him a man of an active and original mind. His originality, indeed, sometimes over-reached the comprehension both of the public and his superiors; he was imprisoned for an attack on the Hanoverian succession which was intended ironically; apparently he was ignorant of what every journalist ought to know that irony is at once the most dangerous and the most ineffectual weapon in the whole armourty of the press. The fertility and ingenuity of his intellect may be best gauged by the number of modern enterprises and contrivances that are foreshadowed in his work. Here are a few, all utterly unknown in his own day, collected by a student of his works; a Board of Trade register for seamen; factories for goods; agricultural credit banks; a commission of enquiry into bankruptcy; and a system of national poor relief. They show him to have been an independent and courageous thinker where social questions were concerned.

He was nearly sixty before he had published his first novel, *Robinson Crusoe*, the book by which he is universally known, and on which with the seven other novels which followed in the foundation of his literary fame rests. But his earlier works—they are reputed to number over two hundred—possess no less remarkable literary qualities. It is not too much to say that all the gifts which are habitually recommended for cultivation by those who aspire to journalistic success are to be found in his prose. He has in the first place the gift of perfect lucidity no matter how complicated the subject he is expounding; such a book as his *Complete English Tradesman* is full of passages in which complex and difficult subject-matter is set forth so plainly and clearly that the least literate of his readers could have no doubt of his understanding it. He has also an amazingly exact acquaintance with the technicalities of all kinds of trades and professions; none of our writers, not even Shakespeare, shows half such a knowledge of the circumstances of life among different ranks and conditions of men; none of them has realized with such fidelity how so many different persons lived and moved. His gift of narrative and description is ;masterly, as readers of his novels know (we shall have to come back to it in discussing the growth of the English novel); several of his works show him to have been endowed with a fine faculty of psychological observation. Without the least consciousness of the value of what he was writing, nor indeed with any deliberate artistic intention, he made himself one of the masters of English prose.

Defoe had been the champion of the Whigs; on the Tory side the ablest pen was that of Jonathan Swift. His works proclaim him to have had an intellect less wide in its range than that of his antagonist but more vigorous and powerful. He wrote, too, more carefully. In his youth he had been private secretary to Sir William Temple, a writer now as good as forgotten because of the triviality of his matter, but in his day esteemed because of the easy urbanity and polish of his prose. From him Swift learned the labour of the file, and he declared in later life that it was "generally believed that this author has advanced our English tongue to as great a perfection as it can well bear." In fact he added to the ease and cadences he had learned from Temple qualities of vigour and directness of his own which put his work far above his master's. And he dealt with more important subject-matter than the academic exercises on which Temple exercised his fastidious and meticulous powers of revision.

In temperament he is opposed to all the writers of his time. There is no doubt but there was some radical disorder in his system; brain disease clouded his intellect in his old age, and his last years were death in life; right through his life he was a savagely irritable, sardonic, dark and violent man, impatient of the slightest contradiction or thwarting, and given to explosive and instantaneous rage. He delighted in flouting convention, gloried in outraging decency. The rage, which, as he said himself, tore his heart out, carried him to strange excesses. There is something ironical (he would himself have appreciated it) in the popularity of *Gulliver's Travels* as a children's book—that ascending wave of savagery and satire which overwhelms policy and learning to break against the ultimate citadel of humanity itself. In none of his contemporaries (except perhaps in the sentimentalities of Steele) can one detect the traces of emotion; to read Swift is to be conscious of intense feeling on almost every page. The surface of his style may be smooth and equable but the central fires of passion are never far beneath, and through cracks and fissures come intermittent bursts of flame. Defoe's irony is so measured and studiously commonplace that perhaps those who imprisoned him because they believed him to be serious are hardly to be blamed; Swift's quivers and reddens with anger in every line.

But his pen seldom slips from the strong grasp of his controlling art. The extraordinary skill and closeness of his allegorical writings—unmatched in their kind—is witness to the care and sustained labour which went to their making. He is content with no general correspondences; his allegory does not fade away into a story in which only the main characters have a secondary significance; the minutest circumstances have a bearing in the satire and the moral. In *The Tale of a Tub* and in *Gulliver's Travels*—particularly in the former—the multitude as well as the aptness of the parallels between the imaginary narrative and the facts it is meant to represent is unrivalled in works of the kind. Only the highest mental powers, working with intense fervour and concentration, could have achieved the sustained brilliancy of the result. "What a genius I had when I wrote that book !" Swift is said to have exclaimed in his old age when he re-read *The Tale of a Tub*, and certainly the book is a marvel of constructive skill, all the more striking because it makes allegory out of history and consequently is denied that freedom of narrative so brilliantly employed in the *Travels*.

Informing all his writings too, besides intense feeling and an omnipresent and controlling art, is strong common sense. His aphorisms, both those collected under the heading of *Thoughts on Various Subjects*, and countless others scattered up and down his pages, are a treasury of sound, if a little sardonic, practical wisdom. His most insistent prejudices foreshadow in their essential sanity and justness those of that great master of life, Dr. Johnson. He could not endure over-politeness, a vice which must have been very oppressive in society of his day. He savagely resented and condemned a display of affection—particularly marital affection—in public. In an age when it was the normal social system of settling quarrels, he condemned duelling; and he said some very wise things—things that might still be said—on modern education. In economics he was as right-hearted as Ruskin and as wrong-headed. Carlyle, who was in so many respects an echo of him, found in a passage in his works a "dim anticipation" of his philosophy of clothes.

The leading literary invention of the period—after that of the heroic couplet for verse—was the prose periodical essay. Defoe, it is hardly necessary to say, began it; it was his nature to be first with any new thing : but its establishment as a prevailing literary mode is due to two authors, Joseph Addison and Richard Steele. Of the two famous series—the *Tatler* and the *Spectator*—for which they were both responsible, Steele must take the first credit; he began them, and though Addison came in and by the deftness and lightness of his writing took the lion's share of their popularity, both the plan and the characters round whom the bulk of the essays in the *Spectator* came to revolve was the creation of his collaborator. Steele we know very intimately from his own writings and from Thackeray's portrait of him. He was an emotional, full-blooded kind of man, reckless and dissipated but fundamentally honest and good-hearted—a type very common in his day as the novels show, but not otherwise to be found in the ranks of its writers. What there is of pathos and sentiment, and most of what there is of humour in the *Tatler* and the *Spectator* are his. And he created the *dramatis personæ* out of whose adventures the slender thread of continuity which binds the essays together is woven. Addison, though less open to the onslaughts of the conventional moralist, was a less lovable personality. Constitutionally endowed with little vitality, he suffered mentally as well as bodily from languor and lassitude. His lack of enthusiasm, his cold-blooded formalism, caused comment even in an age which prided itself in self-command and decorum.

His very malevolence proceeded from a flaccidity which meanly envied the activities and enthusiasms of other men. As a writer he was superficial; he had not the requisite energy for forming a clear or profound judgment on any question of difficulty; Johnson's comment, "He thinks justly but he thinks faintly" sums up the truth about him. His good qualities were of a slighter kind than Swift's; he was a quiet and accurate observer of manners and fashions in life and conversation, and he had the gift of a style—what Johnson calls "The Middle Style"—very exactly suited to the kind of work on which he was habitually engaged, "always equable, always easy, without glowing words or pointed sentences" but polished, lucid, and urbane.

Steele and Addison were conscious moralists as well as literary men. They desired to purge society from Restoration licences; to their efforts we must credit the alteration in morality which *The School for Scandal* shows over *The Way of the World*. Their professed object as they stated themselves was "to banish vice and ignorance out of the territories of Great Britain," (nothing less !) and to bring philosophy out of closets and libraries, schools and colleges, to dwell in clubs and assemblies, at tea-tables and coffee-houses." In fact their satires were politically nearer home, and the chief objects of their aversion were the Tory squires whom it was their business as Whigs to deride. On the Coverley papers in the Spectator rests the chief part of their literary fame; these belong rather to the special history of the novel than to that of the periodical essay.

The Romantic Revival

There are two ways of approaching the periods of change and new birth in literature. The commonest and, for all the study which it entails, the easiest, is that summed up in the phrase, literature begets literature. Following it, you discover and weigh literary influences, the influence of poet on poet, and book on book. You find one man harking back to earlier models in his own tongue, which an intervening age misunderstood or despised; another, turning to the contemporary literatures of neighbouring countries; another, perhaps, to the splendour and exoticism of the east. In the matter of form and style, such a study carries you far. You can trace types of poetry and meters back to curious and unsuspected originals, find the well-known verse of Burns' epistles turning up in Provencal; Tennyson's *In Memoriam* stanza in use by Ben Jonson; the meter of *Christabel* in minor Elizabethan poetry; the peculiar form of Fitzgerald's translation of *Omar Khayyam* followed by so many imitators since, itself to be the actual reflection of the rough metrical scheme of his Persian original. But such a study, though it is profitable and interesting, can never lead to the whole truth. As we saw in the beginning of this book, in the matter of the Renaissance, every age of discovery and re-birth has its double aspect. It is a revolution in style and language, an age of literary experiment and achievement, but its experiments are dictated by the excitement of a new subject-matter, and that subject-matter is so much in the air, so impalpable and universal that it eludes analysis. Only you can be sure that it is this weltering contagion of new ideas, and new thought—the "Zeitgeist," the spirit of the age, or whatever you may call it—that is the essential and controlling force. Literary loans and imports give the forms into which it can be moulded, but without them it would still exist, and they are only the means by which a spirit which is in life itself, and which expresses itself in action, and in concrete human achievement, gets itself into the written word. The romantic revival numbers Napoleon amongst its leaders as well as Byron, Wellington, Pitt and Wilberforce, as well as Keats and Wordsworth. Only the literary manifestations of the time concern us here, but it is important to remember that the passion for simplification and for a return to nature as a refuge from the artificial complexities of society, which inspired the *Lyrical Ballads*, inspired no less the course of the Revolution in France, and later, the destruction by Napoleon of the smaller feudal states of Germany, which made possible German nationality and a national spirit.

In this romantic revival, however, the revolution in form and style matters more than in most. The classicism of the previous age had been so fixed and immutable; it had been enthroned in high places, enjoyed the esteem of society, arrogated to itself the acceptance which good breeding and good manners demanded. Dryden had been a Court poet, careful to change his allegiance with the changing monarchy. Pope had been the equal and intimate of the great people of his day, and his followers, if they did not enjoy the equality, enjoyed at any rate the patronage of many noble lords. The effect of this was to give the prestige social usage to the verse in which they wrote and the language they wrote and the language they used. "There was," said Dr. Johnson, "before the time of Dryden no poetical diction, no system of words at once refined from the grossness of domestic use, and free from the harshness of terms appropriated to particular arts. Words too familiar or too remote to defeat the purpose of a poet." This poetic diction, refined from the grossness of domestic use, was the standard poetic speech of the eighteenth century. The heroic couplet in which it was cast was the standard meter. So that the first object of the revolt of the romantics was the purely literary object of getting rid of the vice of an unreal and artificial manner of writing. They desired simplicity of style.

When the *Lyrical Ballads* of Wordsworth and Coleridge were published in 1798, the preface which Wordsworth wrote as their manifesto hardly touched at all on the poetic imagination or the attitude of the poet to life and nature. The only question is that of diction. "The majority of the following poems," he writes, "are to be considered as experiments. They were written chiefly with a view to ascertain how far the language of conversation in the middle and lower classes of society is adapted to the purposes of poetic pleasure." And in the longer preface to the second edition, in which the theories of the new school on the nature and methods of the poetic imagination are set forth at length, he returns to the same point. "The language too, of these men (that is those in humble and rustic life) has been adopted .... because such men hourly communicate with the best objects from which the best part of language is originally derived, and because from their rank in society, and the sameness and narrow circle of their intercourse, being less under the influence of social vanity, they convey their feelings and notions in simple unelaborated expressions." Social vanity—the armour which we wear to conceal our deepest thoughts and feelings—that was what Wordsworth wished to be rid of, and he chose the language of the common people, not because it fitted, as an earlier school of poets who used the common speech had asserted, the utterance of habitual feeling and common sense, but because it is the most sincere expression of the deepest and rarest passion. His object was the object attained by Shakespeare in some of his supremest moments; the bare intolerable force of the speeches after the murder of Macbeth, or of King Lear's

> "Do not laugh at me,
> For as I am a man, I think this lady
> To be my child Cordelia."

Here, then, was one avenue of revolt from the tyranny of artificiality, the getting back of common speech into poetry. But there was another, earlier and more potent in its effect. The eighteenth century, weary of its own good sense and sanity, turned to the Middle Ages for picturesqueness and relief. Romance of course, had not been dead in all these years, when Pope and Addison made with and good sense the fashionable temper for writing. There was a strong romantic tradition in the eighteenth century, though it does not give its character to the writing of the time. Dr. Johnson was fond of old romances. When he was in Skye he amused himself by thinking of his Scottish tour as the journey of a knight-errant. "These fictions of the Gothic romances," he said, "are not so remote from credibility as is commonly supposed." It is a mistake to suppose that the passion for mediævalism began with either Coleridge or Scott. Horace Walpole was as enthusiastic as either of them; good eighteenth century prelates like Hurd and Percy, found in what they called the Gothic an inexhaustible source of delight. As was natural, what attracted them in the

Middle Ages was not their resemblances to the time they lived in, but the points in which the two differed. None of them had knowledge enough, or insight enough, to conceive or sympathize with the humanity of the thirteenth century, to shudder at its cruelties and hardnesses and persecutions, or to comprehend the spiritual elevation and insight of its rarest minds. "It was art," said William Morris, "art in which all men shared, that made life romantic as people called it in those days. That and not robber barons, and inaccessible kings, with their hierarchy of serving nobles, and other rubbish." Morris belonged to a time which knew its middle ages better. To the eighteenth century the robber barons and the "other rubbish" were the essence of romance. For Percy and his followers, mediævalism was a collection of what actors call "properties" gargoyles, and odds and ends of armour and castle keeps with secret passages, banners and gay colours, and gay shimmering obsolete words. Mistaking what was on its surface at any rate a subtle and complex civilization, for rudeness and quaintness, they seemed to themselves to pass back into a freer air, where any extravagance was possible, and good breeding and mere circumspection and restraint vanished like the wind.

A similar longing to be rid of the precision and order of everyday life drove them to the mountains, and to the literature of Wales and the Highlands, to Celtic, or pseudo-Celtic romance. To the fashion of the time mountains were still frowning and horrid steeps; in Gray's Journal of his tour in the Lakes, a new understanding and appreciation of nature is only struggling through; and when mountains became fashionable, it was at first and remained in part at least, till the time of Byron, for those very theatrical qualities which had hitherto put them in abhorrence. Wordsworth, in his *Lines written above Tintern Abbey*, in which he sets forth the succeeding stages of his mental development, refers to this love of the mountains for their spectacular qualities, as the first step in the progress of his mind to poetic maturity :

" The sounding cataract
Haunted me like a passion; the tall rock,
The mountain and the deep and gloomy wood,
Their colours and their forms were then to me
An appetite."

This same passion for the "sounding cataract" and the "tall rock," this appetite for the deep and gloomy wood, gave its vogue in Wordsworth's boyhood to Macpherson's *Ossian*, a book which whether it be completely fraudulent or not, was of capital importance in the beginnings of the romantic movement.

The love of mediæval quaintness and obsolete words, however, led to a more important literary event—the publication of Biship Percy's edition of the ballads in the Percy folio—the *Reliques of Ancient Poetry*. Percy to his own mind knew the Middle Ages better than they knew themselves, and he took care to dress to advantage the rudeness and plainness of his originals. Perhaps we should not blame him. Sir Walter Scott did the same with better tact and skill in his Border minstrelsy, and how many distinguished editors are there, who have tamed and smoothed down the natural wildness and irregularity of Blake ? But it is more important to observe that when Percy's reliques came to have their influence on writing his additions were imitated as much as the poems on which he grafted them. Chatterton's *Rowley Poems*, which in many places seem almost inconceivably banal and artificial to us today, caught their accent from the episcopal editor as much as from the ballads themselves. None the less, whatever its fault, Percy's collection gave its impetus to one half of the romantic movement; it was eagerly read in Germany, and when it came to influence Scott and Coleridge it did so not only directly, but through Burger's imitation of it; it began the modern study and love of the ballad which has given us *Sister Helen*, the *White Ship*, and the *Lady of Shalott*.

But the romantic revival goes deeper than any change, however momentous of fashion or style. It meant certain fundamental changes in human outlook. In the first place, one notices in the authors of the time an extraordinary development of imaginative sensibility; the mind at its countless points of contact with the sensuous world and the world of thought, seems to become more alive and alert. It is more sensitive to fine impressions, to finely graded shades of difference. Outward objects and philosophical ideas seem to increase in their content and their meaning, and acquire a new power to enrich the intensest life of the human spirit. Mountains and lakes, the dignity of the peasant, the terror of the supernatural, scenes of history, mediæval architecture and armour, and mediæval thought and poetry, the arts and mythology of Greece—all became springs of poetic inspiration and poetic joy. The impressions of all these things were unfamiliar and ministered to a sense of wonder, and by that very fact they were classed as romantic, as modes of escape from a settled way of life. But they were also in a sense familiar too. The mountains made their appeal to a deep implanted feeling in man, to his native sense of his own worth and dignity and splendour as a part of nature, and his recognition of natural scenery as necessary, and in its fullest meaning as sufficient for his spiritual needs. They called him back from the artificiality and complexity of the cities he had built for himself, and the society he had weaved round him, to the natural world in which Providence had planted him of old, and which was full of significance for his soul. The greatest poets of the romantic revival strove to capture and convey the influence of nature on the mind, and of the mind on nature interpenetrating one another. They were none the less artists because they approached nature in a state of passive receptivity. They believed in the autocracy of the individual imagination noneth less because their mission was to divine nature and to understand her, rather than to correct her profusions in the name of art.

In the second place the romantic revival meant a development of the historical sense. Thinkers like Burke and Montesquieu helped students of politics to acquire perspective; to conceive modern institutions not as things separate, and separately created, but as conditioned by, and evolved from, the institutions of an earlier day. Even the revolutionary spirit of the time looked both before and after, and took history as well as the human perfectibility imagined by philosophers into its purview. In France the reformers appealed in the first instance for a States General—a mediæval institution—as the corrective of their wrongs, and later when they could not, like their neighbours in Belgium, demand reform by way of the restoration of their historical rights, they were driven to go a step further back still, beyond history to what they conceived to be primitive society, and demand the rights of man. This development of the historical sense, which had such a widespread influence on politics, got itself into literature in the creation of the historical novel. Scott and Chateaubriand revived the old romance in which by a peculiar ingenuity of form, the adventures of a typical hero of fiction are cast in a historical setting and set about with portraits of real personages. The historical sense affected, too, novels dealing with contemporary life. Scott's best work, his novels of Scottish character, catch more than half their excellence from the richness of colour and proportion which the portraiture of the living people acquires when it is aided by historical knowledge and imagination.

Lastly, besides this awakened historical sense, and this quickening of imaginative sensibility to the message of nature, the Romantic revival brought to literature a revival of the sense of the connection between the visible world and another world which is unseen. The supernatural which in all but the crudest of mechanisms had been out of English literature since *Macbeth*, took hold on the imaginations of authors, and brought with it a new subtlety and a new and nameless horror and fascination. There is nothing in earlier English literature to set beside the strange and terrible indefiniteness of the *Ancient Mariner*, and though much in this kind has been written since, we have not got far beyond the skill and imagination with which Coleridge and Scott worked on the instinctive fears that lie buried in the human mind.

Of all these aspects of the revival, however, the new sensitiveness and accessibility to the influences of external nature was the most pervasive and the most important. Wordsworth speaks for the love that is in homes where poor men lie, the daily teaching that is in

"Woods and rills:
The silence that is in the starry sky,
The peace that is among the lonely hills."

Shelley for the wildness of the west wind, and the ubiquitous spiritual emotion which speaks equally in the song of a skylark or a political revolution. Byron for the swing and roar of the sea. Keats for verdurous glooms and winding mossy ways. Scott and Coleridge, though like Byron they are less with nature than with romance, share the same communion.

This imaginative sensibility of the romantics not only deepened their communion with nature, it brought them into a truer relation with what had before been created in literature and art. The romantic revival is the Golden Age of English criticism; all the poets were critics of one sort or another—either formally in essays and prefaces, or in passing and desultory flashes of illumination in their correspondence. Wordsworth, in his prefaces, in his letter to a friend of Burns which contains such a breadth and clarity of wisdom on things that seem alien to his sympathies, even in some of his poems; Coleridge, in his *Biographia Literaria*, in his notes on Shakespeare, in those rhapsodies at Highgate which were the basis for his recorded table talk; Keats in his letters; Shelley in his *Defence of Poetry;* Byron in his satires and journals. Scott in those lives of the novelists which contain so much truth and insight into the works of fellow craftsmen—they are all to be found turning the new acuteness of impression which was in the air they breathed, to the study of literature, as well as to the study of nature. Alongside of them were two authors, Lamb and Hazlitt, whose bent was rather critical than creative, and the best part of whose intelligence and sympathy was spent on the sensitive and loving divination of our earlier literature. With these two men began the criticism of acting and of pictorial art that have developed since into two of the main kinds of modern critical writing.

Romantic criticism, both in its end and its method, differs widely from that of Dr. Johnson and his school. Wordsworth and Coleridge were concerned with deep-seated qualities and temperamental differences. Their critical work revolved round their conception of the fancy and the imagination, the one dealing with nature on the surface and decorating it with imagery, the other penetrating to its deeper significances. Hazlitt and Lamb applied their analogous conception of wit as a lower quality than humour, in the same fashion. Dr. Johnson looked on the other hand for correctness of form, for the subordination of the parts to the whole, for the self-restraint and good sense which common manners would demand in society, and wisdom in practical life. His school cared more for large general outlines than for truth in detail. They would not permit the idiosyncrasy of a personal or individual point of view : hence they were incapable of understanding lyricism, and they preferred those forms of writing which set themselves to express the ideas and feelings that most men may be supposed to have in common. Dr. Johnson thought a bombastic and rhetorical passage in Congreve's *Mourning Bride* better than the famous description of Dover cliff in *King Lear*. "The crows, sir," he said of the latter, "impede your fall." Their town breeding, and possibly, as we saw in the case of Dr. Johnson, an actual physical disability, made them distrust any clear and sympathetic rendering of the sense impressions which nature creates. One cannot imagine Dr. Johnson caring much for the minute observations of Tennyson's nature poems, or delighting in the verdurous and mossy alleys of Keats. His test in such a case would be simple; he would not have liked to have been in such places, nor reluctantly compelled to go there would he in all likelihood have had much to say about them beyond that they were damp. For the poetry—such as Shelley's—which worked by means of impalpable and indefinite suggestion, he would, one may conceive, have cared even less. New modes of poetry asked of critics new sympathies and a new way of approach. But it is time to turn to the authors themselves.

The case of Wordsworth is peculiar. In his own day he was vilified and misunderstood; poets like Byron, whom most of us would now regard simply as depending from the school he created, sneered at him. Shelley and Keats failed to understand him or his motives; he was suspected of apostasy, and when he became poet laureate he was written off as a turn-coat who had played false to the ideals of his youth. Now common opinion regards him as a poet above all the others of his age, and amongst all the English poets standing beside Milton, but a step below Shakespeare himself—and we know more about him, more about the processes by which his soul moved from doubts to certainties, from troubles to triumph, than we do about any other author we have. This knowledge we have from the poem called, *The Prelude*, which was published after his death. It was designed to be only the opening and explanatory section of a philosophical poem, which was never completed. Had it been published earlier it would have saved Wordsworth from the coldness and neglect he suffered at the hands of younger men like Shelley; it might even have made their work different from what it is. It has made Wordsworth very clear to us now.

Wordsworth is that rarest thing amongst poets, a complete innovator. He looked at things in a new way. He found his subjects in new places; and he put them into a new poetic form. At the turning point of his life, in his early manhood, he made one great discovery, had one great vision. By the light of that vision and to communicate that discovery he wrote his greatest work. By and by the vision faded, the world fell back into the light of common day, his philosophy passed from discovery to acceptance, and all unknown to him his pen fell into a common way of writing. The faculty of reading which has added fuel to the fire of so many waning inspirations was denied him. He was much too self-centered to lose himself in the works of other. Only the shock of a change of environment—a tour in Scotland, or abroad—shook him into his old thrill of imagination, so that a few fine things fitfully illumine the enormous and dreary bulk of his later work. If we lost all but the *Lyrical Ballads*, the poems of 1804, and the *Prelude*, and the *Excursion*, Wordsworth's position as a poet would be no lower than it is now, and he would be more readily accepted by those who still find themselves uncertain about him.

The determining factor in his career was the French Revolution—that great movement which besides re-making French and Europe, made our very modes of thinking anew. While an undergraduate in Cambridge Wordsworth made several vacation visits to France. The first peaceful phase of the Revolution was at its height; France and the assembly were dominated by the little group of revolutionary orators who took their name from the south-western province from which most of them came, and with this group—the Girondists—Wordsworth threw in his lot. Had he remained he would probably have gone with them to the guillotine. As it was, the commands of his guardian brought him back to England, and he was forced to contemplate from a distance the struggle in which he burned to take an active part. One is accustomed to think of Wordsworth as a mild old man, but such a picture if it is thrown back as a presentment of the Wordsworth of the nineties is a far way from the truth. This darkly passionate man tortured himself with his longings and his horror. War came and the prayers for victory in churches found him in his heart praying for defeat; then came the execution of the king; then the plot which slew the Gironde. Before all this Wordsworth trembled as Hamlet did when he learned the ghost's story. His faith in the world was shaken. First his own country had taken up arms against what he believed to be the cause of liberty. Then faction had destroyed his friends whom he believed to be its standard bearers. What was in the world, in religion, in morality that such things could be ? In the face of this tremendous problem, Wordsworth, unlike Hamlet, was resolute and determined. It was, perhaps, characteristic of him that in his desire to get his feet on firm rock again he fled for a time to the exactest of sciences—to mathematics. But though he got certainties there, they must have been, one judges, certainties too arid for his thirsting mind. Then he made his great discovery—helped to it, perhaps, by his sister Dorothy and his friend Coleridge—he found nature, and in nature, peace.

Not a very wonderful discovery, you will say, but though the cleansing and healing force of natural surroundings on the mind is a familiar enough idea in our own day, that is only because Wordsworth found it. When he gave his message to the world it was a new message. It is worth while remembering that it is still an unaccepted one. Most of his critics still consider it only Wordsworth's fun when he wrote :

"One impulse from the vernal wood
Can teach us more of man,
Of moral evil and of good,
Than all the sages can."

Yet Wordsworth really believed that moral lessons and ideas were to be gathered from trees and stones. It was the main part of his teaching. He claimed that his own morality had been so furnished him, and he wrote his poetry to convince other people that what had been true for him could be true for them too.

For him life was a series of impressions, and the poet's duty was to recapture those impressions, to isolate them and brood over them, till gradually as a result of his contemplation emotion stirred again—an emotion akin to the authentic thrill that had excited him when the impression was first born in experience. Then poetry is made; this emotion "recollected" as Wordsworth said (we may add, recreated) "in tranquillity" passes into enduring verse. He treasured numberless experiences of this kind in his own life. Some of them are set forth in the *Prelude*, that for instance on which the poem *The Thorn* in the *Lyrical Ballads* is based; they were one or other of them the occasion of most of his poems; the best of them produced his finest work—such a poem for instance as *Resolution and Independence* or *Gipsies*, where some chance sight met with in one of the poet's walks is brooded over till it becomes charged with a tremendous significance for him and for all the world. If we ask how he differentiated his experiences, which had most value for him, we shall find something deficient. That is to say, things which were unique and precious to him do not always appear so to his readers. He counted as gold much that we regard as dross. But though we may differ from his judgments, the test which he applied to his recollected impressions is clear. He attached most value to those which brought witl them the sense of an indwelling spirit, transfiguring with it: radiance, rocks and fields and trees and the men and womei who lived close enough to them to partake of their strength– the sense, as he calls it in his *Lines above Tintern Abbey* o something "more deeply interfused" by which all nature i: made one. Sometimes, as in the hymn to Duty, it is conceive(as law. Duty before whom the flowers laugh, is the daughte of the voice of God, through whom the most ancient heaven: are fresh and strong. But in most of his poems its ends do no trouble; it is omnipresent; it penetrates everything and trans figures everything; it is God. It was Wordsworth's belief that th perception of this indwelling spirit weakened as age grew. Fo a few precious and glorious years he had the vision

> "When meadow, grove, and stream,
> The earth, and every common sight
> To me did seem
> Apparelled in celestial light,
> The glory and the freshness of a dream."

Then as childhood, when "these intimations of immortality,' this perception of the infinite are most strong, passed furthei and further away, the vision faded and he was left gazing in the light of common day. He had his memories and that was all

There is, of course, more in the matter than this, and Wordsworth's beliefs were inextricably entangled with the conception which Coleridge borrowed from German philosophy.

> "We receive but what we give"

wrote Coleridge to this friend,

> "Add in our life alone doth Nature live."

And Wordsworth came to know that the light he had imagined to be bestowed, was a light reflected from his own mind. It is easy to pass from criticism to metaphysics where Coleridge leads, and wise not to follow.

If Wordsworth represents that side of the Romantic Revival which is best described as the return to Nature, Coleridge has justification for the phrase "Renascence of Wonder." He revived the supernatural as a literary force, emancipated it from the crude mechanism which had been applied to it by dilettantes like Horace Walpole and Mrs. Radcliffe, and invested it instead with that air of suggestion and indefiniteness which gives the highest potency to it in its effect on the imagination. But Coleridge is more noteworthy for what he suggested to others than for what he did in himself. His poetry is, even more than Wordsworth's, unequal; he is capable of large tracts of dreariness and flatness; he seldom finished what he began. The *Ancient Mariner*, indeed, which was the fruit of his close companionship with Wordsworth, is the only completed thing of the highest quality in the whole of his work. *Christabel* is a splendid fragment; for years the first part lay uncompleted and when the odd accident of an evening's intoxication led him to commence the second, the inspiration had fled. For the second part, by giving to the fairy atmosphere of the first a local habitation and a name, robbed it of its most precious quality; what it gave in exchange was something the public could get better from Scott. *Kubla Khan* went unfinished because the call of a friend broke the thread of the reverie in which it was composed. In the end came opium and oceans of talk at Highgate and fouled the springs of poetry. Coleridge never fulfilled the promise of his early days with Wordsworth. "He never spoke out." But it is on the lines laid down by his share in the pioneer work rather than on the lines of Wordsworth's that the second generation of Romantic poets—that of Shelley and Keats—developed.

The work of Wordsworth was conditioned by the French Revolution but it hardly embodied the revolutionary spirit. What he conceived to be its excesses revolted him, and though he sought and sang freedom, he found it rather in the later revolt of the nationalities against the Revolution as manifested in Napoleon himself. The spirit of the revolution, as it was understood in France and in Europe, had to wait for Shelley for its complete expression. Freedom is the breath of his work—freedom not only from the tyranny of earthly powers, but from the tyranny of religion, expressing itself in republicanism, in atheism, and in complete emancipation from the current moral code both in conduct and in writing. The reaction which had followed the overthrow of Napoleon at Waterloo, sent a wave of absolutism and repression all over Europe. Italy returned under the heel of Austria; the Bourbons were restored in France; in England came the days of Castlereagh and Peterloo. The poetry of Shelley is the expression of what the children of the revolution—men and women who were brought up in and believed the revolutionary gospel—thought about these things.

But it is more than that. Of no poet in English, nor perhaps in any other tongue, could it be said with more surety, that the pursuit of the spirit of beauty dominates all his work. For Shelley it interfused all nature and to possess it was the goal of all endeavour. The visible world and the world of thought mingle themselves inextricably in his contemplation of it. For him there is no boundaryline between the two, the one is as real and actual as the other. In his hands that old trick of the poets, the simile, takes on a new and surprising form. He does not enforce the creations of his imagination by the analogy of natural appearances; his instinct is just the opposite—to describe and illumine nature by a reference to the creatures of thought. Other poets, Keats for instance, or Tennyson, or the older poets like Dante and Homer, might compare ghosts flying from an hanter like leaves flying before the wind. They might describe a poet wrapped up in his dreams as being like a bird singing invisible in the brightness of the sky. But Shelley can write of the west wind as

> " Before whose unseen presence the leaves, dead,
> Are driven like ghosts from an enchanter fleeing."

and he can describe a skylark in the heavens as

> " Like a poet hidden
> In the light of thought."

Of all English poets he is the most completely lyrical. Nothing that he wrote but is wrought out of the anguish or joy of his own heart.

> " Most wretched souls,"

he writes

> " Are cradled into poetry by wrong
> They learn in suffering what they teach in song."

Perhaps his work is too impalpable and moves in an air too rarefied. It sometimes lacks strength. It fails to take grip enough of life. Had he lived he might have given it these things; there are signs in his last poems that he would have given it. But he could hardly have battered the sheer and triumphant lyricism of *The Skylark*, of some of his choruses, and of the *Ode to Dejection*, and of the *Lines written on the Eugenean hills*.

If the Romantic sense of the one-ness of nature found its highest exponent in Shelley, the Romantic sensibility to outward impressions reached its climax in Keats. For him life is a series of sensations, felt with almost febrile acuteness. Records of sight and touch and smell crowd every line of his work; the scenery of a garden in Hampstead becomes like a landscape in the tropics, so extraordinary vivid and detailed is his apprehension and enjoyment of what it has to give him. The luxuriance of his sensations is matched by the luxuriance of his powers of expression. Adjectives heavily charged with messages for the senses, crowd every line of his work, and in his earlier poems overlay so heavily the thought they are meant to convey that all sense of sequence and structure is apt to be smothered under their weight. Not that consecutive thought claims a place in his conception of his poetry. His ideal was passive contemplation rather than active mental exertion. "O for a life of sensations rather than of thoughts," he exclaims in one of his letters; and in another, "It is more noble to sit like Jove than to fly like Mercury." His work has one message and one only, the lastingness of beauty and its supreme truth. It is stated in *Endymion* in lines that are worn bare with quotation. It is stated again, at the height of his work in the greatest ode,

> " Beauty is truth, truth beauty : that is all
> We know on earth and all we need to know."

His work has its defects; he died at twentysix so it would be a miracle if it were not so. He lacks taste and measure; he offends by an over-luxuriousness and sensuousness; he fails when he is concerned with flesh and blood; he is apt, as Mr. Robert Bridges has said, "to class women with roses and sweetmeats." But in his short life he attained with surprising rapidity and completeness to poetic maturity, and perhaps from no other poet could we find things to match his greatest—*Hyperion*, *Isabella*, the *Eve of St. Agnes* and the *Odes*.

There remains a poet over whom opinion is more sharply divided than it is about any other writer in English. In his day Lord Byron was the idol, not only of his countrymen, but of Europe. Or all the poets of the time he was, if we except Scott, whose vogue he eclipsed, the only one whose work was universally known and popular. Everybody read him; he was admired not only by the multitude and by his equals, but by at least one who was his superior, the German poet Goethe, who did not hesitate to say of him that he was the greatest talent of the century. Though this exalted opinion still persists on the

Continent, hardly anyone could be found in England to subscribe to it now. Without insularity, we may claim to be better judges of authors in our own tongue than foreign critics, however distinguished and comprehending. How then shall be explained Lord Byron's instant popularity and the position he won ? What were the qualities which gave him the power he enjoyed ?

In the first place he appealed by virtue of his subject-matter—the desultory wanderings of *Childe Harold* traversed ground every mile of which was memorable to men who had watched the struggle which had been going on in Europe with scarcely a pause for twenty years. Descriptive journalism was then and for nearly half a century afterwards unknown, and the poem by its descriptiveness, by its appeal to the curiosity of its readers, made the same kind of success that vividly written special correspondence would to-day, the charm of meter super-added. Lord Byron gave his readers something more, too, than mere description. He added to it the charm of a personality, and when that personality was enforced by a title, when it proclaimed its sorrows as the age's sorrows endowed itself with an air of symbolism and set itself up as a kind of scapegoat for the nation's sins, its triumph was complete. Most men have from time to time to resist the temptation to pose to themselves; many do not even resist it. For all those who chose to believe themselves blighted by pessimism, and for all the others who would have loved to believe it, Byron and his poetry came as an echo of themselves. Shallow called to shallow. Men found in him, as their sons found more reputably in Tennyson, a picture of what they conceived to be the state of their own minds.

But he was not altogether a man of pretence. He really and passionately loved freedom; no one can question his sincerity in that. He could be a find and scathing satirist; and though he was careless, he had great poetic gifts.

The age of the Romantic Revival was one of poetry rather than of prose; it was in poetry that the best minds of the time found their means of expression. But it produced prose of rare quality too, and there is delightful reading in the works of its essayists and occasional writers. In its form the periodical essay had changed little since it was first made popular by Addison and Steele. It remained, primarily, a vehicle for the expression of a personality, and it continued to seek the interests of its readers by creating or suggesting an individuality strong enough to carry off any desultory adventure by the mere force of its own attractiveness. Yet there is all the difference in the world between Hazlitt and Addison, or Lamb and Steele. The *Tatler* and the *Spectator* leave you with a sense of artifice; Hazlitt and Lamb leave you with a grip of a real personality—in the one case very vigorous and combative, in the other set about with a rare plaintiveness and gentleness, but in both absolutely sincere. Addison is gay and witty and delightful but he only plays at being human; Lamb's essays—the translation into print of a heap of idiosyncrasies and oddities, and likes and dislikes, and strange humours—come straight and lovably from a human soul.

The prose writers of the romantic movement brought back two things into writing which had been out of it since the seventeenth century. They brought back egotism and they brought back enthusiasm. They had the confidence that their own tastes and experiences were enough to interest their readers; they mastered the gift of putting themselves on paper. But there is one wide difference between them and their predecessors. Robert Burton was an egotist but he was an unconscious one; the same is, perhaps, true though much less certainly of Sir Thomas Browne. In Lamb and Hazlitt and De Quincey egotism was deliberate, consciously assumed, the result of a compelling and shaping art. If one reads Lamb's earlier essays and prose pieces one can see the process at work—watch him consciously imitating Fuller, or Burton, or Browne, mirroring their idiosyncrasies, making their quaintnesses and graces his own. By the time he came to write the *Essays of Elia*, he had mastered the personal style so completely that his essays seem simply the overflow of talk. They are so desultory; they move from one subject to another so waywardly—such an essay as a *Chapter on Ears*, for instance, passing with the easy inconsequence of conversation from anatomy through organ music to beer—when they quote, as they do constantly, it is incorrectly, as in the random reminiscences of talk. Here one would say is the cream risen to the surface of a full mind and skimmed at one taking. How far all this is from the truth we know—know, too, how for months he polished and rewrote these magazine articles, rubbing away roughnesses and corners, taking off the traces of logical sequences and argument, till in the finished work of art he mimicked inconsequence so perfectly that his friends might have been deceived. And the personality he put on paper was partly an artistic creation, too. In life Lamb was a nervous, easily excitable and emotional man; his years were worn with the memory of a great tragedy and the constantly impending fear of a repetition of it. One must assume him in his way to have been a good man of business—he was a clerk in the India House, then a throbbing centre of trade, and the largest commercial concern in England, and when he retired his employers gave him a very handsome pension. In the early portrait by Hazlitt there is a dark and gleaming look of fire and decision. But you would never guess it from his books. There he is the gentle recluse, dreaming over old books, old furniture, old prints, old plays and playbills; living always in the past, loving in the town secluded by ways like the Temple, or the libraries of Oxford Colleges, and in the country quiet and shaded lanes, none of the age's enthusiasm for mountains in his soul. When he turned critic it was not to discern and praise the power and beauty in the works of his contemporaries but to rediscover and interpret the Elizabethan and Jacobean romantic plays.

This quality of egotism Lamb shares with other writers of the time, with De Quincey, for instance, who left buried in work which is extensive and unequal, much that lives by virtue of the singular elaborateness and loftiness of the style which he could on occasion command. For the revival of enthusiasm one must turn to Hazlitt, who brought his passionate and combative disposition to the service of criticism, and produced a series of studies remarkable for their earnestness and their vigour, and for the essential justness which they display despite the prejudice on which each of them was confessedly based.

The Victorian Age

Had it not been that with two exceptions all the poets of the Romantic Revival died early, it might be more difficult to draw a line between their school and that of their successors than it is. As it happened, the only poet who survived and wrote was Wordsworth, the oldest of them all. For long before his death he did nothing that had one touch of the fire and beauty of his earlier work. The respect he began, after a lifetime of neglect, to receive in the years immediately before his death, was paid not to the conservative laureate of 1848, but to the revolutionary in art and politics of fifty years before. He had lived on long after his work was done

> "To hear the world applaud the hollow ghost
> That blamed the living man."

All the others, Keats, Shelley, Byron were dead before 1830, and the problem which might have confronted us had they lived, of adult work running counter to the tendencies and ideals of youth, does not exist for us Keats or Shelley might have lived as long as Carlyle, with whom they were almost exactly contemporary; had they done so, the age of the Romantic Revival and the Victorian age would have been united in the lives of authors who were working in both. We should conceive that is, the whole period as one, just as we conceive of the Renaissance in England, from Surrey to Shirley, as one. As it is, we have accustomed ourselves to a strongly marked line of division. A man must be on either one side or the other; Wordsworth, though he wrote on till 1850, is on the further side, Carlyle, though he was born in the same year as Keats, on the hither side. Still the accident of length of days must not blind us to the fact that the Victorian period, though in many respects its ideals and modes of thinking differed from those of the period which preceded it, is essentially an extension of the Romantic Revival and not a fresh start. The coherent inspiration of romanticism disintegrated into separate lines of development, just as in the seventeenth century the single inspiration of the Renaissance broke into different schools. Along these separate lines represented by such men as Browning, the Pre-Raphaelites, Arnold, and Meredith, literature enriched and elaborated itself into fresh forms. None the less, every author in each of these lines of literary activity invites his readers to understand his direct relations to the romantic movement. Rossetti touches it through his original, Keats; Arnold through Goethe and Byron; Browning first through Shelley and then in item after item of his varied subject-matter.

In one direction the Victorian age achieved a salient and momentous advance. The Romantic Revival had been interested in nature, in the past, and in a lesser degree in art, but it had not been interested in men and women, To Wordsworth the dalesmen of the lakes were part of the scenery they moved in; he saw men as trees walking, and when he writes about them as in such great poems as *Resolution and Independence*, the *Brothers*, or *Michael*, it is as natural objects he treats them, invested with the lonely remoteness that separates them from the complexities and passions of life as it is lived. They are there, you feel, to teach the same lesson as the landscape teaches in which they are set. The passing of the old Cumberland beggar through villages and past farmsteads, brings to those who see him the same kind of consolation as the impulses from a vernal wood that Wordsworth celebrated in his purely nature poetry. Compare with Wordsworth, Browning, and note the fundamental change in the attitude of the poet that his work reveals. *Pippa Passes* is a poem on exactly the same scheme as the *Old Cumberland Beggar*, but in treatment no two things could be further apart. The intervention of Pippa is dramatic, and though her song is in the same key as the wordless message of Wordsworth's beggar she is a world apart from him, because she is something not out of natural history, but out of life. The Victorian age extended the imaginative sensibility which its predecessor had brought to bear on nature and history, to the complexities of human life. It searched for individuality in character, studied it with a loving minuteness, and built up out of its discoveries amongst men and women a body of literature which in its very mode of conception was more closely related to life, and thus the object of greater interest and excitement to its readers, than anything which had been written in the previous ages. It is the direct result of this extension of romanticism that the novel became the characteristic means of literary expression of the time, and that Browning, the poet who more than all others represents the essential spirit of his age, should have been as it were, a novelist in verse. Only one other literary form, indeed, could have ministered adequately to this awakened interest, but by some luck not easy to understand, the drama, which might have done with greater economy and directness the work the novel had to do, remained outside the main stream of literary activity. To the drama at last it would seem that we are returning, and it may be that in the future the direct representation of the clash of human life which is still mainly in the hands of our novelists, may come back to its own domain.

The Victorian age then added humanity to nature and art as the subject-matter of literature. But it went further than that. For the first time since the Renaissance, came an era which was conscious of itself as an epoch in the history of mankind, and confident of its mission. The fifteenth and sixteenth centuries revolutionised cosmography, and altered the face of the physical world. The nineteenth century, by the discoveries of its men of science, and by the remarkable and rapid succession of inventions which revolutionized the outward face of life, made hardly less alteration in accepted ways of thinking. The evolutionary theory, which had been in the air since Goethe, and to which Darwin was able to give an incontrovertible basis of scientific fact, profoundly influenced man's attitude to nature and to religion. Physical as apart from natural science made scarcely less advance, and instead of a world created in some fixed moment of time, on which had been placed by some outward agency all the forms and shapes of nature that we know, came the conception of a planet we know, came the conception of a planet congealing out of a nebula, and of some lower, simpler and primeval form of life multiplying and diversifying itself through succeeding stages of development to form both the animal and the vegetable world. This conception not only enormously excited and stimulated thought, but it gave thinkers a strange sense of confidence and certainty not possessed by the age before. Everything seemed plain to them; they were heirs of all the ages. Their doubts were as certain as their faith.

> "There lives more faith in honest doubt
> Believe me than in half the creeds."

said Tennyson; "honest doubt," hugged with all the certainty of a revelation, is the creed of most of his philosophical poetry, and what is more to the point was the creed of the masses that were beginning to think for themselves, to whose awakening interest his work so strongly appealed. There were no doubt, literary side-currents. Disraeli survived to show that there were still young men who thought Byronically. Rossetti and his school held themselves proudly aloof from the rationalistic and scientific tendencies of the time, and found in the Middle ages, better understood than they had been either by Coleridge or Scott, a refuge from a time of factories and fact. The Oxford movement ministered to the same tendencies in religion and philosophy; but it is the scientific spirit, and all that the scientific spirit implied, its certain doubt, its care for minuteness, and truth of observation, its growing interest in social processes, and the conditions under which life is lived, that is the central fact in Victorian literature.

Tennyson represents more fully than any other poet this essential spirit of the age. If it be true, as has been often asserted, that the spirit of an age is to be found best in the work of lesser men, his complete identity with the thought of his time is in itself evidence of his inferiority to his contemporary, Browning. Comparison between the two men seem inevitable: they were made by readers when *In Memoriam* and *Men and Women* came hot from the press, and they have been made ever since. There could of course, scarcely be two men more dissimilar, Tennyson elaborating and decorating the obvious; Browning delving into the esoteric and the obscure, and bringing up strange and unfamiliar finds; Tennyson in faultless verse registering current newly accepted ways of thought; Browning in advance thinking afresh for himself, occupied ceaselessly in the arduous labour of creating an audience fit to judge him. The age justified the accuracy with which Tennyson mirrored it, by accepting him and rejecting Browning. It is this very accuracy that almost forces us at this time to minimize and dispraise Tennyson's work. We have passed from Victorian certainties, and so he is apt when he writes in the mood of *Locksley Hall* and the rest, to appear to us a little shallow, a little empty, and a little pretentious.

His earlier poetry, before he took upon himself the burden of the age, is his best work, and it bears strongly marked upon it the influence of Keats. Such a poem for instance as *Œnone* shows an extraordinarily fine sense of language and melody, and the capacity caught from Keats of conveying a rich and highly coloured pictorial effect. No other poet, save Keats, has had a sense of colour so highly developed as Tennyson's. From his boyhood he was an exceedingly close and sympathetic observer of the outward forms of nature, and he makes a splendid use of what his eyes had taught him in these earlier poems. Later his interest in insects and birds and flowers outran the legitimate opportunity he possessed of using it in poetry. It was his habit, his son tells us, to keep note books of things he had observed in his garden or in his walks, and to work them up afterwards into similes for the *Princess* and the *Idylls of the King*. Read in the books written by admirers, in which they have been studied and collected (there are several of them) these similes are pleasing enough: in the text where they stand they are apt to have the air of impertinences, beautiful and extravagant impertinences no doubt, but alien to their setting. In one of the *Idylls of the King* the fall of a drunken knight from his horse is compared to the fall of a jutting edge of cliff and with it a lance-like fir-tree, which Tennyson had observed near his home, and one cannot resist the feeling that the comparison is a thought too great for the thing it was meant to illustrate. So, too, in the Princess when he describes a hand-writing,

> "In such a hand as when a field of corn
> Bows all its ears before the roaring East."

he is using up a sight noted in his walks and transmuted into poetry on a trivial and frivolous occasion. You do not feel, in fact, that the handwriting visualized spontaneously called up the comparison; you are as good as certain that the simile existed waiting for use before the handwriting was thought of.

The accuracy of his observation of nature, his love of birds and larvæ is matched by the carefulness with which he embodies, as soon as ever they were made, the discoveries of natural and physical science. Nowadays, possibly because these things have become commonplace to us, we may find him a little school-boy-like in his pride of knowledge. He knows that

> "This world was once a fluid haze of light,
> Till toward the centre set the starry tides
> And eddied wild suns that wheeling cast
> The planets."

just as he knows what the catkins on the willows are like, or the names of the butterflies : but he is capable, on occasion of "dragging it in," as in

> "The nebulous star we call the sun,
> If that hypothesis of theirs be sound."

from the mere pride in his familiarity with the last new thing. His dealings with science, that is, no more than his dealings with nature, have that inevitableness, that spontaneous appropriateness that we feel we have a right to ask from great poetry.

Had Edgar Allan Poe wanted an example for his theory of the impossibility of writing, in modern times, a long poem, he might have found it in Tennyson. His strength is in his shorter pieces; even where as in *In Memoriam* he has conceived and written something at once extended and beautiful, the beauty lies rather in the separate parts; the thing is more in the nature of a sonnet sequence than a continuous poem. Of his other larger works, the *Princess*, a scarcely happy blend between burlesque in the manner of the *Rape of the Lock*, and a serious apostleship of the liberation of women, is solely redeemed by these lyrics. Tennyson's innate conservatism hardly squared with the liberalising tendencies he caught from the more advanced thought of his age, in writing it. Something of the same kind is true of *Maud*, which is a novel told in dramatically varied verse. The hero is morbid, his social satire peevish, and a story which could have been completely redeemed by the ending (the death of the hero), which artistic fitness demands, is of value for us now through its three amazing songs, in which the lyric genius of Tennyson reached its finest flower. It cannot be denied, either, that he failed—though magnificently—in the *Idylls of the King*. The odds were heavily against him in the choice of a subject. Arthur is at once too legendary and too shadowy for an epic hero, and nothing but the treatment that Milton gave to Satan (i.e. flat substitution of the lengendary person by a newly created character) could fit him for the place. Even if Arthur had been more promising than he is, Tennyson's sympathies were fundamentally alien from the moral and religious atmosphere of Arthurian romance. His robust Protestantism left no room for mysticism; he could neither appreciate nor render the mystical fervour and exultation which is in the old history of the Holy Grail. Nor could he comprehend the morality of a society where courage, sympathy for the oppressed, loyalty and courtesy were the only essential virtues, and love took the way of freedom and the heart rather than the way of law. In his heart Tennyson's attitude to the ideals of chivalry and the old stories in which they are embodied differed probably very little from that of Roger Ascham, or of any other Protestant Englishman; when he endeavoured to make an epic of them and to fasten to it an allegory in which Arthur should typify the war of soul against sense, what happened was only what might have been expected. The heroic enterprise failed, and left us with a series of mid-Victorian novels in verse in which the knights figure as heroes of the generic mid-Victorian type.

But if he failed in his larger poems, he had a genius little short of perfect in his handling of shorter forms. The Arthurian story which produced only middling moralizing in the *Idylls*, gave us as well the supremely written Homeric episode of the *Morte d'Arthur*, and the sharp and defined beauty of *Sir Galahad* and the *Lady of Shallott*. Tennyson had a touch of the pre-Raphaelite faculty of minute painting in words, and the writing of these poems is as clear and naïve as in the best things of Rossetti. He had also what neither Rossetti nor any of his contemporaries in verse, except Browning, had, a find gift of understanding humanity. The peasants of his English idylls are conceived with as much breadth of sympathy and richness of humour, as purely and as surely, as the peasants of Chaucer or Burns. A note of passionate humanity is indeed in all his work. It makes vivid and intense his scholarly handling of Greek myth; always the unchanging human aspect of it attracts him most, in Œnone's grief, in the indomitableness of Ulysses, the weariness and disillusionment in Tithonus. It has been the cause of the comfort he has brought to sorrow; none of his generation takes such a human attitude to death. Shelley could yearn for the infinite, Browning treat it as the last and greatest adventure, Arnold meet it clear eyed and resigned. To Wordsworth it is the mere return of man the transient to Nature the eternal.

> "No motion has she now; no force,
> She neither hears nor sees,
> Rolled round in earth's diurnal course
> With rocks and stones and trees."

To Tennyson it brings the fundamental human home-sickness for familiar things.

> "Ah, sad and strange as on dark summer dawns,
> The earliest pipe of half-awakened birds
> To dying ears when unto dying eyes
> The casement slowly grows a glimmering square."

It is an accent which wakes an echo in a thousand hearts.

While Tennyson, in his own special way and, so to speak, in collaboration with the spirit of the age, was carrying on the work of Romanticism on its normal lines, Browning was finding a new style and a new subject matter. In his youth he had begun as an imitator of Shelley, and *Pauline* and *Paracelsus* remain to show what the influence of the "sun-treader" was on his poetry. But as early as his second publication, *Bells and Pomegranates*, he had begun to speak for himself, and with *Men and Women*, a series of poems of amazing variety and brilliance, he placed himself unassailably in the first rank. Like Tennyson's, his genius continued high and undimmed while life was left him. *Men and Women* was followed by an extraordinary narrative poem, *The Ring and the Book*, and it by several volumes of scarcely less brilliance, the last of which appeared on the very day of his death.

Of the two classes into which, as we saw when we were studying Burns, creative artists can be divided, Browning belongs to that one which makes everything new for itself, and has in consequence to educate the readers by whom its work can alone be judged. He was an innovator in nearly everything he did; he thought for himself; he wrote for himself, and in his own way. And because he refused to follow ordinary modes of writing, he was and is still widely credited with being tortured and obscure. The charge of obscurity is unfortunate because it tends to shut off from his a large class of readers for whom he has a sane and special and splendid message.

His most important innovation in form was his device of the dramatic lyric. What interested him in life was men and women, and in them, not their actions, but the motives which governed their actions. To lay bare fully the working of motive in a narrative form with himself as narrator was obviously impossible; the strict dramatic form, though he attained some success in it, does not seem to have attracted him, probably because in it the ultimate stress must be on the thing done rather than the thing thought; there remained, therefore, of the ancient forms of poetry, the lyric. The lyric had of course been used before to express emotions imagined and not real to the poet himself; Browning was the first to project it to express imagined emotions of men and women, whether typical or individual, whom he himself had created. Alongside this perversion of the lyric, he created a looser and freer form, the dramatic monologue, in which most of his most famous poems, *Cleon, Sludge the Medium, Bishop Blougram's Apology*, etc. are cast. In the convention which Browning established in it, all kinds of people are endowed with a miraculous articulation, a new gift of tongues; they explain themselves, their motives, the springs of those motives (for in Browning's view every thought and act of a man's life is part of an interdependent whole), and their author's peculiar and robust philosophy of life. Out of the dramatic monologues he devised the scheme of *The Ring and the Book*, a narrative poem in which the episodes, and not the plot, are the basis of the structure, and the story of a trifling and sordid crime is set forth as it appeared to the minds of the chief actors in succession. To these new forms he added the originality of an extraordinary realism in style. Few poets have the power by a word, a phrase, a flash of observation in detail to make you see the event as Browning makes you see it.

Many books have been written on the philosophy of Browning's poetry. Stated briefly its message is that of an optimism which depends on a recognition of the strenuousness of life. The base of his creed, as of Carlyle's, is the gospel of labour; he believes in the supreme moral worth of effort. Life is a "training school" for a future existence, and our place in it depends on the courage and strenuousness with which we have laboured here. Evil is in the world only as an instrument in the process of development; by conquering it we exercise our spiritual faculties the more. Only torpor is the supreme sin, even as in *The Statue and the Bust* where effort would have been to a criminal end.

> "The counter our lovers staked was lost
> As surely as if it were lawful coin :
> And the sin I impute to each frustrate ghost
> Was, the unlit lamp and the ungirt loin,
> Though the end in sight was a crime, I say."

All the other main ideas of his poetry fit with perfect consistency on to his scheme. Love, the manifestation of a man's or a woman's nature, is the highest and most intimate relationship possible, for it is an opportunity—the highest opportunity—for spiritual growth. It can reach this end though an actual and earthly union is impossible.

> "She has lost me, I have gained here:
> Her soul's mine and thus grown perfect,
> I shall pass my life's remainder.
> Life will just hold out the proving
> Both our powers, alone and blended;
> And then come the next life quickly!
> This world's use will have been ended."

It follows that the reward of effort is the promise of immortality, and that for each man, just because his thoughts and motives taken together count, and not one alone, there is infinite hope.

The contemporaries of Tennyson and Browning in poetry divide themselves into three separate schools. Nearest to them in temper is the school of Matthew Arnold and Clough; they have the same quick sensitiveness to the intellectual tendencies of the age, but their foothold in a time of shifting and dissolving creeds is a stoical resignation very different from the buoyant optimism of Browning, or Tennyson's mixture of science and doubt and faith. Very remote from them on the other hand is the backward-gazing mediævalism of Rossetti and his circle, who revived (Rossetti from Italian sources, Morris from Norman) a Middle age which neither Scott nor Coleridge had more than partially and brokenly understood. The last school, that to which Swinburne and Meredith with all their differences unite in belonging, gave up Christianity with scarcely so much as a regret,

> " We have said to the dream that caress'd and the
>   dread that smote us,
> Good-night and good-bye."

and turned with a new hope and exultation to the workship of our immemorial mother the earth. In both of them, the note of enthusiasm for political liberty which had been lost in Wordsworth after 1815, and was too early extinguished with Shelley, was revived by the Italian Revolution in splendour and fire.

As one gets nearer one's own time, a certain change comes insensibly over one's literary studies. Literature comes more and more to mean imaginative literature or writing about imaginative literature. The mass of writing comes to be taken not as literature, but as argument or information; we consider it purely from the point of view of its subject matter. A comparison will make this at once clear. When a man reads Bacon, he commonly regards himself as engaged in the study of English literature; when he reads Darwin he is occupied in the study of natural science. A reader of Bacon's time would have looked on him as we look on Darwin now.

The distinction is obviously illogical, but a writer on English literature within brief limits is forced to bow to it if he wishes his book to avoid the dreariness of a summary, and he can plead in extenuation the increased literary output of the later age, and the incompleteness with which time so far has done its work in sifting the memorable from the forgettable, the ephemeral from what is going to last. The main body of imaginative prose literature—the novel—is treated of in the next chapter and here no attempt will be made to deal with any but the admittedly greatest names. Nothing can be said, for instance, of that fluent journalist and biassed historian Macaulay, nor of the mellifluousness of Newman, nor of the vigour of Kingsley or Maurice; nor of the writings, admirable in their literary qualities of purity and terseness, of Darwin or Huxley; nor of the culture and apostleship of Matthew Arnold. These authors, one and all, interpose no barrier, so to speak, between their subject-matter and their readers; you are not when you read them conscious of a literary intention, but of some utilitarian one, and as an essay on English literature is by no means a handbook to serious reading they will be no more mentioned here.

In the case of one nineteenth century writer in prose, this method of exclusion cannot apply. Both Carlyle and Ruskin were professional men of letters; both in the voluminous compass of their works touched on a large variety of subjects; both wrote highly individual and peculiar styles; and both without being either professional philosophers or professional preachers, were as every good man of letters, whether he denies it or not, is and must be, lay moralists and prophets. Of the two Ruskin is plain and easily read, and he derives his message; Carlyle, his original, is apt to be tortured and obscure. Inside the body of his work the student of nineteenth century literature is probably in need of some guidance; outside so far as prose is concerned he can fend for himself.

As we saw, Carlyle was the oldest of the Victorians; he was over forty when the Queen came to the throne. Already his years of preparation in Scotland, town and country, were over, and he had settled in that famous little house in Chelsea which for nearly half a century to come was to be one of the central hearths of literary London. More than that, he had already fully formed his mode of thought and his peculiar style. *Sartor Resartus* was written and published serially before the Queen came to the throne; the *French Revolution* came in the year of her accession at the very time that Carlyle's lectures were making him a fashionable sensation; most of his miscellaneous essays had already appeared in the reviews. But with the strict Victorian era, as if to justify the usually arbitrary division of literary history by dynastic periods, there came a new spirit into his work. For the first time he applied his peculiar system of ideas to contemporary politics. *Chartism* appeared in 1839; *Past and Present*, which does the same thing as *Chartism* in an artistic form, three years later. They were followed by one other book—*Latter Day Pamphlets*—addressed particularly to contemporary conditions, and by two remarkable and voluminous historical works. Then came the death of his wife, and for the last fifteen years of his life silence, broken only briefly and at rare intervals.

The reader who comes to Carlyle with preconceived notions based on what he has heard of the subject-matter of his books is certain to be surprised by what he finds. There are histories in the canon of his works and pamphlets on contemporary problems, but they are composed on a plan that no other historian and no other social reformer would own. A reader will find in them no argument, next to no reasoning, and little practical judgment. Carlyle was not a great "thinker" in the strictest sense of that term. He was under the control, not of his reason, but of his emotions; deep feeling, a volcanic intensity of temperament flaming into the light and heat of prophecy, invective, derision, or a simple splendour of eloquence, is the characteristic of his work. Against cold-blooded argument his passionate nature rose in fierce rebellion; he had no patience with the formalist or the doctrinaire. Nor had he the faculty of analysis; his historical works are a series of pictures of tableaux, splendidly and vividly conceived, and with enormous colour and a fine illusion of reality, but one sided as regards the truth. In his essays on hero-worship he contents himself with a noisy reiteration of the general predicate of heroism; there is very little except their names and the titles to differentiate one sort of hero from another. His picture of contemporary conditions is not so much a reasoned indictment as a wild and fantastic orgy of epithets : "dark simmering pit of Tophet," "bottomless universal hypocrisies," and all the rest. In it all he left no practical scheme. His works are fundamentally not about politics or history or literature, but about himself. They are the exposition of a splendid egotism, fiercely enthusiastic about one or two deeply held convictions; their strength does not lie in their matter of fact.

This is, perhaps, a condemnation of him in the minds of those people who ask of a social reformer an acutarially accurate scheme for the abolition of poverty, or from a prophet a correct forecast of the result of the next general election. Carlyle has little help for these and no message save the disconcerting one of their own futility. His message is at once larger and simpler, for though his form was prose, his soul was a poet's soul, and what he has to say is a poet's word. In a way, it is partly Wordsworth's own. The chief end of life, his message is, is the performance of duty, chiefly the duty of work. "Do thy little stroke of work; this is Nature's voice, and the sum of all the commandments, to each man." All true work is religion, all true work is worship; to labour is to pray. And after work, obedience the best discipline, so he says in *Past and Present*, for governing, and "our universal duty and destiny; wherein whose will not bend must break." Carlyle asked of every man, action and obedience and to bow to duty; he also required of him sincerity and veracity, the duty of being a real and not a sham, a strenuous warfare against cant. The historical facts with which he had to deal he grouped under these embracing categories, and in the *French Revolution*, which is as much a treasure-house of his philosophy as a history, there is hardly a page on which they do not appear. "Quack-ridden," he says, "in that one word lies all misery whatsoever."

These bare elemental precepts he clothes in a garment of amazing and bizarre richness. There is nothing else in English faintly resembling the astonishing eccentricity and individuality of his style. Gifted with an extraordinarily excitable and vivid imagination; seeing things with sudden and tremendous vividness, as in a searchlight or a lightning flash, he contrived to convey to his readers his impressions full charged with the original emotion that produced them, and thus with the highest poetic effect. There is nothing in all descriptive writing to match the vividness of some of the scenes in the *French Revolution* or in the narrative part of *Cromwell's Letters and Speeches*, or more than perhaps in any of his books, because in it he was setting down deep-seated impressions of his boyhood rather than those got from brooding over documents, in *Sartor Resartus*. Alongside this unmatched pictorial vividness and a quite amazing richness and rhythm of language, more surprising and original than anything out of Shakespeare, there are of course, striking defects—a wearisome reiteration of emphasis, a clumsiness of construction, a saddening fondness for solecisms and hybrid inventions of his own. The reader who is interested in these (and every one who reads him is forced to become so) will find them faithfully dealt with in John Sterling's remarkable letter (quoted in Carlyle's *Life of Sterling*) on *Sartor Resartus*. But gross as they are, and frequently as they provide matter for serious offence, these eccentricities of language link themselves up in a strange indissoluble way with Carlyle's individuality and his power as an artist. They are not to be imitated, but he would be much less than he is without them, and they act by their very strength and pungency as a preservative of his work. That of all the political pamphlets which the new era of reform occasioned, his, which were the least in sympathy with it and are the furthest off the main stream of our political thinking now, alone continue to be read, must be laid down not only to the prophetic fervour and fire of their inspiration but to the dark and violent magic of their style.

The Novel

The faculty for telling stories is the oldest artistic faculty in the world, and the deepest in planted in the heart of man. Before the rudest cave-pictures were scratched on the stone, the story-teller, it is not unreasonable to suppose, was plying his trade. All early poetry is simply story-telling in verse. Stories are the first literary interest of the awakening mind of a child. As that is so, it is strange that the novel, which of all literary ways of story-telling seems closest to the unstudied tale-spinning of talk, should be the late discovery that it is. Of all the main forms into which the literary impulse moulds the stuff of imagination, the novel is the last to be devised. The drama dates from prehistoric times, so does the epic, the ballad and the lyric. The novel, as we know it, dates practically speaking from 1740. What is the reason it is so late in appearing ?

The answer is simply that there seems no room for good drama and good fiction at the same time in literature; drama and novels cannot exist side by side, and the novel had to wait for the decadence of the drama before it could appear and triumph. If one were to make a table of succession for the various kinds of literature as they have been used naturally and spontaneously (not academically), the order would be the epic, the drama, the novel; and it would be obvious at once that the order stood for something more than chronological succession, and that literature in its function as a representation and criticism of life passed from form to form in the search of greater freedom, greater subtlety, and greater power. At present we seem to be at the climax of the third stage in this development; there are signs that the fourth is on the way, and that it will be a return to drama, not to the old, formal, ordered kind, but, something new and freer, ready to gather up and interpret what there is of newness and freedom in the spirit of man and the society in which he lives.

The novel, then, had to wait for the drama's decline, but there was literary story-telling long before that. There were mediæval romances in prose and verse; Renaissance pastoral tales, and stories of adventure; collections, plenty of them, of short stories like Boccaccio's, and those in Painter's *Palace of Pleasure*. But none of these, not even romances which deal in moral and sententious advice like *Euphues*, approach the essence of the novel as we know it. They are all (except *Euphues*, which is simply a framework of travel for a book of aphorisms) simple and objective; they set forth incidents or series of incidents; long or short they are anecdotes only—they take no account of character. It was impossible we should have the novel as distinct from the tale, till stories acquired a subjective interest for us; till we began to think about character and to look at actions not only outwardly, but within at their springs.

As has been stated early in this book, it was in the seventeenth century that this interest in character was first wakened. Shakespeare had brought to the drama, which before him was concerned with actions viewed outwardly, a psychological interest; he had taught that "character is destiny," and that men's actions and fates spring not from outward agencies, but from within in their own souls. The age began to take a deep and curious interest in men's lives; biography was written for the first time and autobiography; it is the great period of memoir-writing both in England and France; authors like Robert Burton came, whose delight it was to dig down into human nature in search for oddities and individualities of disposition; humanity as the great subject of enquiry for all men, came to its own. All this has a direct bearing on the birth of the novel. One transient form of literature in the seventeenth century—the Character—is an ancestor in the direct line. The collections of them—*Earle's Microcosmography* is the best—are not very exciting reading, and they never perhaps quite succeeded in naturalizing a form borrowed from the later age of Greece, but their importance in the history of the novel to come is clear. Take them and add them to the story of adventure—*i.e.*, introduce each fresh person in your plot with a description in the character form, and the step you have made towards the level is enormous; you have given to plot which was already there, the added interest of character.

That, however, was not quite how the thing worked in actual fact. At the heels of the "Character" came the periodical essay of Addison and Steele. Their interest in contemporary types was of the same quality as Earle's or Hall's, but they went a different way to work. Where these compressed and cultivated style which was staccato and epigrammatic, huddling all the traits of their subject in short sharp sentences that follow each other with all the brevity and curtness of items in a prescription, Addison and Steele observed a more artistic plan. They made, as it were, the prescription up, adding on ingredient after another slowly as the mixture dissolved. You are introduced to Sir Roger de Coverley, and to a number of other typical people, and then in a series of essays which if they were disengaged form their setting would be to all intents a novel and a fine one, you are made aware one by one of different traits in his character and those of his friends, each trait generally enshrined in an incident which illustrates it; you get to know them, that is, gradually, as you would in real like, and not all in a breath, in a series of compressed statements, as is the way of the character writers. With the Coverely essays in the *Spectator*, the novel in one of tis forms—that in which an invisible and all knowing narrator tells a story in which some one else whose character he lays bare for us is the hero—is as good as achieved.

Another manner of fiction—the autobiographical—had already been invented. It grew directly out of the public interest in autobiography, and particularly in the tales of their voyages which the discovers wrote and published on their return form their voyages which the discoverers wrote adventures. Its establishment in literature was the work of two authors, Bunyan and Defoe. The books of Bunyan, whether they are told in the first person or no, are and were meant to be autobiographical; their interest is a subjective interest. Here is a man who endeavours to interest you, not in the character of some other person he has imagined or observed, but in himself. His treatment of it is characteristic of the awakening talent for fiction of his time. *The Pilgrim's Progress* is begun as an allegory, and so continues for a little space till the story takes hold of the author. When it does, whether he knew it or not, allegory goes to the winds. But the autobiographical form of fiction in its highest art is the creation of Defoe. He told stories of adventure, incidents modelled on real life as many tellers of tales had done before him, but to the form as he found it he super-added a psychological interest—the interest of the character of the narrator. He contrived to observe in his writing a scrupulous and realistic fidelity and appropriateness to the conditions in which the story was to be told. We learn about Crusoe's island, for instance, gradually just as Crusoe learns of it himself, though the author is careful by taking his narrator up to a high point of vantage the day after his arrival, that we shall learn the essentials of it, as long as verisimilitude is not sacrificed, as soon as possible. It is the paradox of the English novel that these our earliest efforts in fiction were meant, unlike the romances which preceded them, to pass for truth. Defoe's *Journal of the Plague Year* was widely taken as literal fact, and it is still quoted as such occasionally by rash though reputable historians. So that in the novel began with realism as it has culminated, and across two centuries Defoe and the "naturalists" join hands. Defoe, it is proper also in this place to notice, fixed the peculiar form of the historical novel. In his *Memories of a Cavalier*, the narrative of an imaginary person's adventures in a historical setting is interspersed with the entrance of actual historical personages, exactly the method of historical romancing which was brought to perfection by Sir Walter Scott.

In the eighteenth century came the decline of the drama for which the novel had been waiting. By 1660 the romantic drama of Elizabeth's time was dead; the comedy of the Restoration which followed, witty and brilliant though it was, reflected a society too licentious and artificial to secure it permanence; by the time of Addison play-writing had fallen to journey-work, and the theatre to openly expressed contempt. When Rich Ardson and Fielding published their novels there was nothing to compete with fiction in the popular taste. It would seem as though the novel had bene waiting for this favourable circumstance. In a sudden burst of prolific inventiveness, which can be paralleled in all letters only by the period of Marlowe and Shakespeare, masterpiece after masterpiece poured from the press. Within two generations, besides Richardson and Fielding came Sterne and Goldsmith and Smollett and Fanny Burney in naturalism, and Horace Walpole and Mrs. Radcliffe in the new way of romance. Novels by minor authors were published in thousands as well. The novel, in fact, besides being the occasion of literature of the highest class, attracted by its lucrativeness that under-current of journey-work authorship which had hitherto busied itself in poetry or plays. Fiction has been its chief occupation ever since.

Anything like a detailed criticism or even a bare narrative of this voluminous literature is plainly impossible without the limits of a single chapter. Readers must go for it to books on the subject. It is possible here merely to draw attention to those authors to whom the English novel as a more or less fixed form is indebted for its peculiar characteristics Foremost amongst these are Richardson and Fielding; after them there is Walter Scott. After him, in the nineteenth century, Dickens and Meredith and Mr. Hardy; last of all the French realists and the new school of romance. To one or other of these originals all the great authors in the long list of English novelists owe their method and their choice of subject-matter.

With Defoe fiction gained verisimilitude, it ceased to deal with the incredible; it aimed at exhibiting, though in strange aimed at exhibiting, though in strange and memorable circumstances, the working of the ordinary mind. It is Richardson's main claim to fame that he contrived a form of novel which exhibited an ordinary mind working in normal circumstances, and that he did this with a minuteness which till then had never been thought of and has not since bene surpassed. His talent is very exactly a microscopical talent; 'under it the common stuff of life separated from its surroundings and magnified beyond previous knowledge, yields strange and new and deeply interesting sights. He carried into the study of character which had begun in Addison with an eye to externals and eccentricities, a minute faculty of inspection which watched and recorded unconscious mental emotional processes.

To do this he employed a method which was, in effect, a compromise between that of the autobiography, and that of the tale told by an invisibie narrator. The weakness of the autobiography is that it can write only of events within the knowledge of the supposed speaker, and that consequently the presentation of all but one of the characters of the book is an external presentation. We know, that is, of Man Friday only what Crusoe could, according to realistic appropriateness, tell us about him. We do not know what be thought or felt within himself. On the other hand the method of invisible narration had not at his time acquired the faculty which it possesses now of doing. Friday's thinking aloud or exposing fully the working of his mind. So that Richardson, whose interests were psychological, whose strength and talent lay in the presentation of the states of mind appropriate to situations of passion or intrigue, had to look about him for a new form, and that form he found in the novel be the presentation not of action, but of the springs of action; if the external event is in it always of less importance than the emotions which conditioned it, and the emotions which it set working, the novel of letters is the supreme manner for fiction. Consider the possibilities of it; there is a series of events in which A, B, and C are concerned. Not only can the outward events be narrated as they appeared to all three separately by means of letters from each to another, or to a fourth party, but the motives of each and the emotions which each experiences as a result of the actions of the others or them all, can be laid bare. No other method can wind itself so completely into the psychological intricacies and recesses which lie behind every event. Yet the form, as everybody knows, has not been popular; even an expert novel-reader could hardly name off-hand more than two or three examples of it since Richardson's day. Why is this? Well, chiefly it is because the mass of novelists have not had Richardson's knowledge of, or interest in, the psychological under side of life, and those who have, as, amongst the moderns, Henry James have devised out of the convention of the invisible narrator a method by which they can with greater economy attain in practice fairly good results. For the mere narration of action in which the study of character plays a subsidiary part, it was, of course, from the beginning impossible. Scott turned aside at the height of his power to try it in "Red gauntlet" ; he never made a second attempt.

For Richardson's purpose, it answered admirably, and he used it with supreme effect. Particularly he excelled in that side of the novelist's craft which has ever since (whether because the started it or not) proved the subtlest and most attractive, the presentation of women. Richardson was one of those men who are not at their ease in other men's society, and whom other men, to put it plainly, are apt to regard as coxcombs and fools. But he had a genius for the friendship and confidence of women. In his youth he wrote love letters for them. His first novel grew out of a plan to exhibit in a series of letters the equality of feminine virtue, and in its essence (though with a ludicrous, and so to speak "Kitchen-maidish" misunderstanding of his own sex) adheres to the plan. His second novel, which designs to set up a model man against the monster of iniquity in *Pamela*, is successful only so far as it exhibits the thoughts and feelings of the heroine whom he ultimately marries. His last, *Clarissa Harlowe*, is masterpiece of sympathetic divination into the feminine mind. *Clarissa* is, as has been well said, the "eve of fiction, the prototype of the modern heroine"; feminine psychology as good as unknown before (Shakespeare's women being the "Fridays" of a highly intelligent Crusoe) has hardly been brought further since. But *Clarissa* is more than mere psychology: whether she represents a contemporary tendency or whether Richardson made her so, she starts a new epoch. "This," says Henley, "is perhaps her finest virtue as it is certainly her greatest charm, that until she set the example, woman in literature as a self-suffering individuality, as an existence endowed with equal rights to independence—of choice, volition, action—with man had not begun to be." She had not begun to be it in life either.

What Richardson did for the subtlest part of a novelist's business, his dealings with psychology, Fielding did for the most necessary part of it, the telling of the story. Before him hardly any story had been told well; even if it had been plain and clear as in Bunyan and Defoe it had lacked the emphasis, the light and shade of skilful grouping. On the "picaresque" (so the autobiographical form was called abroad) convention of a journey he grafted a structure based in its outline on the form of the ancient epic. It proved extraordinarily suitable for his purpose. Not only did it make it easy for him to lighten his narrative with excursions in a heightened style, burlesquing his origins, but it gave him at once the right attitude to his material. He told his story as one who knew everything; could tell conversations and incidents as he conceived them happening, with no violation of credibility, nor any strain on his reader's imagination, and without any impropriety could interpose in his own person, pointing things to the reader which might have escaped his attention, pointing at parallels he might have missed, laying bare the irony or humour beneath a situation. He allowed himself digressions and episodes, told separate tales in the middle of the action, introduced, as in Partridge's visit to the theatre, the added piquancy of topical allusion; in fact he did anything he chose. And he laid down that free form of the novel which is characteristically English, and from which, in its essence, no one till the modern realists had made a serious departure.

In the matter of his novels, he excels by reason of a Shakespearean sense of character and by the richness and rightness of his faculty of humour. He had a quick eye for contemporary types, and an amazing power of building out of them men and women whose individuality is full and rounded. You do not feel as you do with Richardson that his fabric is spun silk-worm-wise out of himself; on the contrary you know it to be the fruit of a gentle and observant nature, and a stock of fundamental human sympathy. His gallery of portraits, Joseph Andrews, Parson Adams, Parson Trulliber, Jones, Blifil, Partridge, Sophia and her father and all the rest are each of them minute studies of separate people; they live and move according to their proper natures; they are conceived not from without but from within. Both Richardson and fielding were conscious of a moral intention; but where Richardson is sentimental vulgar, and moral only so far as it is moral (as in *Pamela*), to inculcate selling at the highest price or (as in *Grandison*) to avoid temptations which never come in your way, Fielding's morality is fresh and healthy, and (though not quite free from the sentimentality of scoundrelism) at bottom sane and true. His knowledge of the world kept him right. His acquaintance with life is wide, and his insight is keen and deep. His taste is almost as catholic as Shakespeare's own, and the life he knew, and which other men knew, he handles for the first time with the freedom and imagination of an artist.

Each of the two—Fielding and Richardson —had his host of followers. Abroad Richardson won immediate recognition; in France Diderot went so far as to compare him with Homer and Moses! He gave the first impulse to modern French fiction. At home, less happily, he set going the sentimental school,. and it was only when that had passed away that—in the delicate and subtle character study of Miss Austen—his influence comes to its own. Miss Austen carried a step further, and with an observation which was first hand and seconded by intuitive knowledge, Richardson's analysis of the feminine mind, adding to it a delicate and finely humorous feeling for character in both sexes which was all her own. Fielding's imitators (they number each in his own way, and with his own graces or talent added his rival Smollett, Sterne, and Goldsmith) kept the way which leads to Thackeray and Dickens— the main road of the English Novel.

That road was widened two ways by Sir Walter Scott. The historical novel, which had been before his day either an essay in anachronism with nothing historical in it but the date, or a laborious and uninspired compilation of antiquarian research, took form and life under his hands. His wide reading, stored as it was in a marvelously retentive memory, gave him all the background he needed to achieve a historical setting, and allowed him to concentrate his attention on the actual telling of his story; to which his genial and sympathetic humanity and his quick eye for character gave a humorous depth and richness that was all his own. It is not surprising that he made the historical novel a literary vogue all over Europe. In the second place, he began in his novels of Scottish character a sympathetic study of nationality. He is not, perhaps, a fair guide to contemporary conditions; his interests were too romantic and too much in the past to catch the rattle of the looms that caught the ear of Galt, and if we want a picture of the great fact of modern Scotland, its industrialisation, it is to Galt we must go. But in his comprehension of the essential character of the people he has no rival; in it his historical sense seconded his observation, and the two mingling gave us the pictures whose depth of colour and truth make his Scottish novels, *Old Mortality*, *The Antiquary*, *Redgauntlet*, the greatest things of their kind in literature.

The peculiarly national style of fiction founded by Fielding and carried on by his followers reached its culminating point in *Vanity* Fair. In it the reader does not seen to be simply present at the unfolding of a plot the end of which is constantly present to the mind of the author and to which he is always consciously working, every incident having a bearing on the course of the action; rather he feels himself to be the spectator of a piece of life which is too large and complex to be under the control of a creator, which moves to its close not under the impulsion of a directing hand, but independently impelled by causes evolved in the course of its happening. With this added complexity goes a more frequent interposition of the author in his own person—one of the conventions as we have seen of this national style. Thackeray is present to his reader's attention to the events on which he lays stress, and makes them a starting-point for his own moralising. This persistent moralizing—sham cynical, real sentimental—this thumping of deathbed pillows as in the dreadful case of miss Crawley, makes Thackeray's use of the personal interposition almost less effective than that of any other novelist. Already while he was doing it, Dickens had conquered the public; and the English novel was making its second fresh start.

He is an innovator in more ways than one. In the first place he is the earliest novelist to practise a conscious artistry of plot. *The Mystery of Edwin Drood* remains mysterious, but those who essay to conjecture the end of that unfinished story have at last the surety that its end, full worked out in all its details, had been in its author's mind before he set pen to paper. His imagination was as diligent and as disciplined as his pen. Dickens' practice in this matter could not be better put than in his own words, when he describes himself as "in the first stage of a new book, which consists in going round and round the idea, as you see a bird in his cage go about and about his sugar before he touches it." That his plots are always highly elaborated is the fruit of this preliminary disciplined exercise of thought. The method is familiar to many novelists now; Dickens was the first to put it into practice. In the second place he made a new departure by his frankly admitted didacticism and by the skill with which in all but two or three of his books—*Bleak House*, perhaps, and *Little Dorrit*—he made the discovery which has made him immortal. In him for the first time the English novel produced an author who dug down into the masses of the people for his subjects; apprehended them in all their inexhaustible character and humour and pathos, and reproduced them with a lively and loving artistic skill.

Dickens had, of course, serious faults. In particular, readers emancipated by lapse of time from the enslavement of the first enthusiasm, have quarrelled with the mawkishness and sentimentality of his pathos, and with the exaggeration of his studies of character. It has been said of him, as it has of

Thackeray, that he could not draw a "good woman" and that Agnes Copperfield, like Amelia Sedley, is a very doll-like type of person. To critics of this kind it may be retorted that though "good" and "bad" are categories relevant to melodrama, they apply very ill to serious fiction, and that indeed to the characters of any of the novelists—the Brontes, Mrs. Gaskell or the like—who lay bare character with fullness and intimacy, they could not well be applied at all. The faultness of them in Dickens is less than in Thackeray, for in Dickens they are only incident to the scheme, which lies in the hero (his heroes are excellent) and in the grotesque characters whereas in his rival they are in the theme itself. For his pathos, not even his warmest admirer could perhaps offer a satisfactory case. The charge of exaggeration however is another matter. To the person who complains that he has never met Dick Swiveller or Micawber or Mrs. Gamp the answer is simply Turner's to the sceptical critic of his sunset, "Don't you wish you could?" To the other, who objects more plausibly to Dickens's habit of attaching to each of his characters some label which is either so much flaunted all through that you cannot see the character at all or else mysteriously and unaccountably disappears when the story begins to grip the author, Dickens has himself offered an amusing and convincing defence. In the preface to *Pickwick* he answers those who criticised the novel on the ground that Pickwick began by being purely ludicrous and developed into a serious and sympathetic individuality, by pointing to the analogous process which commonly takes place in actual human relationships. You begin a new acquaintanceship with perhaps not very charitable prepossessions; these later a deeper and better knowledge removes, and where you have before seen an idiosyncrasy you come to love a character. It is ingenious and it helps to explain Mrs. Nickleby, the Pecksniff daughters, and many another. Whether it is true or not (and it does not explain the faultiness of such pictures as Carker and his kind) there can be no doubt that this trick in Dickens of beginning with a salient impression and working outward to a fuller conception of character is part at least of the reason of his enormous hold upon his readers. No man leads you into the mazes of his invention so easily and with such a persuasive hand.

The great novelists who were writing contemporarily with him—the Brontës, Mrs. Gaskell, George Eliot—it is impossible to deal with here, except to say that the last is indisputably, because of her inability to fuse completely art and ethics, inferior to Mrs. Gaskell or to either of the Brontë sisters. Nor of the later Victorians who added fresh variety to the national style can the greatest, Meredith, be more that mentioned for the exquisiteness of his comic spirit and the brave gallery of English men and women he has given us in what is, perhaps, fundamentally has given us in what is, perhaps, fundamentally the most English thing in fiction since Fielding wrote. For our purpose Mr. Hardy, though he is a less brilliant artist, is more to the point. His novels brought into England the contemporary pessimism of Schopenhaur and the Russians, and found a home for it among the English peasantry, Convinced that in the upper classes character could be studied and portrayed only subjectively because of the artificiality of a society which prevented its outlet in action, he turned to the peasantry because with them conduct is the direct expression of the inner life. Character could be shown working, therefore, not subjectively but in the act, if you chose a peasant subject. His philosophy, expressed in this medium, is sombre. In his novels you can trace a gradual realization of the defects of natural laws and the quandary men are put to by their operation. Chance, and irritating and trifling series of coincidences, plays the part of fate. Nature seems to enter with the hopelessness of man's mood. Finally the novelist turns against life itself. "Birth," he says, speaking of Tess, "seemed to her an ordeal of degrading personal compulsion whose gratuitousness nothing in the result seemed to justify and at best could only palliate." It is strange to find pessimism in a romantic setting; strange, too, to find a paganism which is so little capable of light or joy.

The characteristic form of English fiction, that in which the requisite illusion of the complexity and variety of life is rendered by discursiveness, by an author's licence to digress, to double back on himself, to start may be in the middle of a story and work subsequently to the beginning and the end; in short by his power to do whatever is most expressive of his individuality, found a rival in the last twenty years of the nineteenth century in the French Naturalistic or Realist school, in which the illusion of life is got by a studied and sober veracity of statement, and by the minute accumulation of detail. To the French Naturalists a novel approached in importance the work, of a man of science, and they believed it ought to be based on documentary evidence, as a scientific work would be. Above all it ought not to allow itself to be coloured by the least gloss of imagination or idealism; it ought never to shrink form a confrontation of the baked fact. On the contrary it was its business to carry it to the dissecting table and there minutely examine everything that lay beneath its surface.

The school first became an English possession in the early translations of the work of Zola: its methods were transplanted into English fiction by. George Moore. From his novels, both in passages of direct statement and in the light of his practice, it is possible to gather together the materials of manifesto of the English naturalistic school. The naturalists complained that English fiction lacked construction in the strictest sense; they found in the English novel a remarkable absence of organic wholeness; it did not fulfil their first and broadest canon of subject matter—by which a novel has to deal in the first place with a single and rhythmical series of events; it was too discursive. They made this charge against English fiction; they also retorted the charge brought by native writers and their readers against the French of foulness, sordidness and pessimism in their view of life. "We do not," says a novelist in one of Moore's books, "we do not always choose what you call unpleasant subjects, but we do try to get to the roots of things; and the basis of life being material and not spiritual, the analyst sooner or later finds himself invariably handling what this sentimental age calls coarse." "The novel," says the same character, "if it be anything is contemporary history, and exact and complete reproduction of the social surroundings of the age we live in." That succinctly is the naturalistic theory of the novel as a work of science—that as the history of a nation lies hidden often in social wrongs and in domestic grief as much as in the movements of parties or dynasties, the novelist must do for the former what the historian does for the latter. It is his business in the scheme of knowledge of his time.

But the naturalists believed quite as profoundly in the novel as a work of art. They claimed for their careful pictures of the grey and sad and sordid and artistic worth, varying in proportion to the intensity of the emotion in which the picture was composed and according to the picture's truth, but in its essence just as real and permanent as the artistic worth of romance. "Seen from afar," writes Moore, " all things in nature are of equal worth; and the meanest things, when viewed with the eyes of God, are raised to heights of tragic awe which conventionality would limit to the death of kings and patriots." On such a lofty theory they built their treatment and their style. It is a mistake to suppose that the realist school deliberately cultivates the sordid or shocking. Examine in this connection Mr. Moore's *Mummer's Wife*, our greatest English realist novel, and for the matter of that one of the supreme things in English fiction, and you will see that the scrupulous fidelity of the author's method, though it denies him those concessions to a sentimentalist or romantic view of life which are the common implements of fiction, denies him no less the extremities of horror or loathsomeness. The heroine sinks into the miserable squalor of a dipsomaniac and dies from a drunkard's disease, but her end is shown as the ineluctable consequence of her life, its early greyness and monotony, the sudden shock of a new and strange environment and the resultant weakness of will which a morbid excitability inevitably brought about. The novel, that is to say, deals with a "rhythmical series of events and follows them to their conclusion"; it gets at the roots of things; it tells us of something which we know to be true in life whether we care to read it in fiction or not. There is nothing in it of sordidness for sordidness' sake nor have the realists nay philosophy of an unhappy ending. In this case the ending in unhappy because the sequence of events admitted of no other solution; in others the ending is happy or merely neutral as the preceding story decides. If what one may call neutral endings predominate, it is because they also—notoriously—predominate in life. But the question of unhappiness or its opposite has nothing whatever to do with the larger matter of beauty; it is the triumph of the realists that at their best they discovered a new beauty in things, the loveliness that lies in obscure places, the splendour of sordidness, humility, and pain. They have taught us that beauty, life the Spirit, blows where it lists and we know from them that the antithesis between realism and idealism is only on their lower levels; at their summits they unite and are one. No true realist but is an idealist too.

Most of what is best in English fiction since has been directly occasioned by their work; Gissing and Mr. Arnold Bennett may be mentioned as two authors who are fundamentally realist in their conception of the art of the novel, and the realist ideal partakes in a greater or less degree in the work of nearly all our eminent novelists to-day. But realism is not and cannot be interesting to the great public; it portrays people as they are, not as they would like to be, and where they are, not where they would like to be. It gives no background for day-dreaming. Now literature (to repeat what has been than more once stated earlier in this book) is a way of escape from life as well as an echo or mirror of it, and the novel as the form of literature which more than any other men read for pleasure, is the main avenue for this escape. So that alongside this invasion of realism it is not strange that there grew a revival in romance.

The main agent of it, Robert Louis Stevenson, had the romantic strain in him intensified by the conditions under which he worked; a weak and anæmic man, he loved bloodshed as a cripple loves athletics—passionately and with the intimate enthusiasm of make believe which an imaginative man can bring to bear on the contemplation of what can never be his. His natural attraction for "redness and juice" in life was seconded by a delightful and fantastic sense of the boundless possibilities of romance in every-day things. To a realist a hansom-cab driver is a man who makes twenty-five shillings a week, lives in a back street in Pimlico, has a wife who drinks and children who grow up with an alcoholic taint; the realist will compare his lot with other cab-drivers, and find what part of his life is the product of the cab-driving environment, and on that basis he will write his book. To Stevenson and to the romanticist generally, a hansom can-driver is a mystery be-hind whose apparent commonplaceness lie magic possibilities beyond all telling; not one but may be the agent of the Prince of Bohemia, ready to drive you off to some mad and magic adventure in a street which is just as commonplace to the outward eye as the cab-driver himself, but which implicates by its very deceitful commonness whole volumes of romance. The novel-reader to whom *Demos* was the repetition of what he had seen and known, and what had planted sickness in his soul, found the *New Arabian Nights* a refreshing miracle. Stevenson had discovered that modern London had its possibilities of romance. To these two elements of his romantic equipment must be added a third—travel. Defoe never left England, and other early romanticists less gifted with invention than he wrote from the mind's eye and form books. To Stevenson, and to his successor Kipling, whose "discovery" of India is one of the salient facts of modern English letters, and to Conrad belongs the credit of teaching novelists to draw on experience for the scenes they seek to present. A fourth element in the equipment of modern romanticism—that which draws its effects from the "miracles" of modern science, has been added since by H.G. Wells, in whose latest work the realistic and romantic school seem to have united.

The Present Age

We have carried out study down to the death of Ruskin and included in it authors like Swindburne and Meredith who survived till recently; and in discussing the novel we have included men like Kipling and Hardy—living authors,. It would be possible and perhaps safer to stop there and make no attempt to bring writers later than these into our survey. To do so is to court an easily and quickly stated objection. One is anticipating the verdict of posterity. How can we who are contemporaries tell whether an author's work is permanent or no?

Of course, in a sense the point of view expressed by these questions is true enough. It is always idle to anticipate the verdict of posterity. Remember Matthew Arnold's prophecy that at the end of the nineteenth century Wordsworth and Byron would be the two great names in Romantic poetry. No notion is so destructive to the formation of a sound literary taste as the notion that books become literature only when their authors are dead. Round us men and women are putting into plays and poetry and novels the best that they can or know. They are writing not for a dim and uncertain future but for us, and on our recognition and welcome they depend sometimes for their livelihood, always for the courage which carries them on to fresh endeavour. Literature is an ever-living and continuous thing, and we do it less than its due service if we are so occupied reading Shakespeare and Milton and Scott that we have no time to read Yeats, Shaw or Wells. Students of literature must remember that classics are being manufactured daily under their eyes, and that on their sympathy and comprehension depends whether an author receives the success he merits when he is alive to enjoy it.

The purpose of this chapter, then, is to draw a rough picture of some of the lines or schools of contemporary writing—of the writing mainly, though not altogether, of living authors. It is intended to indicate some characteristics of the general trend or drift of literary effort as a whole. The most remarkable feature of the age, as far as writing is concerned, is without doubt its inattention to poetry. Tennyson was a popular author; his books sold in thousands; his lines passed into that common conversational currency of unconscious quotation which is the surest testimony to the permeation of a poet's influence. Even Browning, though his popularity came late, found himself carried into all the nooks and corners of the reading public. His robust and masculine morality, understood at last, or expounded by a semipriestly class of interpreters, made him popular with those readers—and they are the majority—who love their reading to convey a moral lesson; just as Tennyson's reflection of his time's distraction between science and religion endeared them to those who found in him an answer or at least an echo to their own perplexities. A work widely different from either of these, Fitzgerald's *Rubaiyat of Omar Khayyam*, shared and has probably exceeded their popularity for similar reasons. Its easy pessimism and cult of pleasure, its appeal to the indolence and moral flaccidity which is implicit in all men, all contributed to its immense vogue; and among a people who perhaps did not fully understand it but were merely lulled by its sonorousness, a knowledge of it has passed for the insignia of a love of literature and the possession of literary taste. But after Fitzgerald—who? What poet has commanded the ear of the reading public or even a fraction of it? Not Swinburne certainly, partly because of his undoubted difficulty, partly because of a suspicion held of his moral and religious tenets, largely from material reasons quite unconnected with the quality of his work; not Morris, nor his followers; none of the so-called minor poets whom we shall notice presently—poets who have drawn the moods that have nourished their work from the decadents of France. Probably the only writer of verse who is at the same time a poet and has acquired a large popularity and public influence is Kipling. His work as a novelist we mentioned in the last chapter. It remains to say something of his achievements in verse.

Let us grant at once his faults. He can be violent, and over-rhetorical; he labours you with sense impressions, and with the polysyllable rhetoric he learned from Swinburne—and (though this is not the place for a discussion of political ideas) he can offend by the sentimental brutalism which too often passes for patriotism in his poetry. Not that this last represents the total impression of his attitude as an Englishman. His later work in poetry and prose, devoted to the reconstruction of English history, is remarkable for the justness and saneness of its temper. There are other faults—a lack of sureness in taste is one—that could be mentioned but they do not affect the main greatness of his work. He is great because he discovered a new subject-matter, and because of the white heat of imagination which in his best things be brought to bear on it and by which he transposed it into poetry. It is Kipling's special distinction that the apparatus of modern civilization—steam engines, and steamships, and telegraph lines, and the art of fight—take on in his hands a poetic quality as authentic and inspiring as any that ever was cast over the implements of other and what the mass of men believe to have been more picturesque days. Romance is in the present, so he teaches us, not in the past, and we do it wrong to leave it only the territory we have ourselves discarded in the advance of the race. That and the great discovery of India—an India, misunderstood for his own purposes no doubt, but still the first presentiment of an essential fact in our modern history as a people—give him the hold that he has, and rightly, over the minds of his readers.

It is in a territory poles apart from Kipling's that the main stream of romantic poetry flows. Apart from the gravely delicate and scholarly work of. Bridges, and the poetry of some others who work separately away from their fellows, English romantic poetry has concentrated itself into one chief school—the school of the "celtic Revival" of which the leader is W.B. Yeats. Two sources went to its making. In its inception, it arose out of a group of young poets who worked in a conscious imitation of the methods of the French decadents; chiefly of Baudelaire and Verlaine. As a whole their work was merely imitative and not very profound, but each of them—Ernest Dowson and Lionel Johnson, who are both now dead, and others who are still living—produced enough to show that they had at their command a vein of poetry that might have deepened and proved more rich had they gone on working it. One of them W.B. Yeats, by his birth and his reading in Irish legend and folklore, became possessed of a subject-matter denied to his fellows, and it is from the combination of the mood of the decadents with the dreaminess and mystery of Celtic tradition and romance—a combination which came to pass in his poetry—that the Celtic school has sprung. In a sense it has added to the territory explored by Coleridge and Scott and Morris a new province. Only nothing could be further from the objectivity of these men, than the way in which the Celtic school approaches its material. Its stories are clear to itself, it may be, but not to its readers. Deirdre and Conchubar, and Angus and Maeve and Dectora and all the shadowy figures in them scarcely become embodied. Their lives and deaths and loves and hates are only a scheme on which they weave a delicate and dim embroidery of pure poetry—of love and death and old age and the passing of beauty and all the sorrows that have been since the world began and will be till the world ends. If Kipling is of the earth earthy, if the clangour and rush of the world is in everything he writes, Yeats and his school live consciously sequestered and withdrawn, and the world never breaks in on their ghostly troubles or their peace. Poetry never fails to relate itself to its age; if it is not with it, it is against it; it is never merely indifferent. The poetry of these men is the denial, passionately made, of everything the world prizes. While such denial is sincere, as in the best of them, then the verses they make are true and fine. But when it is assumed, as in some of their imitators, then the work they did is not true poetry.

But the literary characteristic of the present age—the one which is most likely to differentiate it from its predecessor, is the revival of the drama. When we left it before the Commonwealth the great English literary school of playwriting—the romantic drama—was already dead. It has had since no second birth. There followed after it the heroic tragedy of Dryden and Shadwell—a turgid, declamatory form of art without importance—and two brilliant comic periods, the earlier and greater that of Congreve and Wycherley, the later more sentimental with less art and vicacity that of Goldsmith and Sheridan. With Sheridan the drama as a literary force died a second time. It has been born again only in our own day. It is, of course, unnecessary to point out that the writing of plays did not cease in the interval; it never does cease. The production of dramatic journey-work has been continuous since the re-opening of the theatres in 1660, and it is carried on as plentifully as ever at this present time. Only side by side with it there has grown up a new literary drama, and gradually the main stream of artistic endeavour which for nearly a century has preoccupied itself with the novel almost to the exclusion of other forms of art, has turned back to the stage as its channel to articulation and an audience. An influence from abroad set it in motion. The plays of Ibsen—produced, the best of them, in the eighties of last century—came to England in the nineties. In a way, perhaps, they were misunderstood by their worshippers hardly less than by their enemies, but all excrescences of enthusiasm apart they taught men a new and freer approach to moral questions, and a new and freer dramatic technique. Where plays had been constructed on a journeyman plan evolved by Labiche and Sardoumid-nineteenth century writers in France—a plan delighting in symmetry, close-jointedness, false correspondences, an impossible use of coincidence, and a quite unreal complexity and elaboration, they become bolder and less artificial, more close to the likelihoods of real life. The gravity of the problems with which they set themselves to deal heightened their influence. In England men began to ask themselves whether the theatre here too could not be made an avenue towards the discussion of living difficulties, and then arose the new school of dramatists—of whom the first and most remarkable is George Bernard Shaw. In his earlier plays he set himself boldly to attack established conventions, and to ask his audiences to think for themselves. *Arms and the Man* dealt a blow at the cheap romanticism with which a peace-living public invests the profession of arms; *The Devil's Disciple* was a shrewd criticism of the preposterous self-sacrifice on which melodrama, which is the most popular non-literary form of play-writing, is commonly based; *Mrs. Warren's Profession* made a brave and plain-spoken attempt to drag the public face to face with the nauseous realities of prostitution; *Widowers' Houses* laid bare the sordidness of a Society which bases itself on the exploitation of the poor for the luxuries of the rich. It took Shaw close on ten years to persuade even the moderate number of men and women who make up a theatre audience that his plays were worth listening to. But before his final success came he had attained a substantial popularity with the public which reads. Possibly his early failure on the stage—mainly due to the obstinacy of playgoers immersed in a stock tradition—was partly due also to his failure in constructive power. He is an adept at tying knots and impatient of unravelling them; his third acts are apt either to evaporate in talk or to find some unreal and unsatisfactory solution for the complexity he has created. But constructive weakness apart, his amazing brilliance and fecundity of dialogue ought to have given him an immediate and lasting grip of the stage. There has probably never been a dramatist who could invest conversation with the same vivacity and point, the same combination of surprise and inevitableness that distinguishes his best work.

Alongside of Shaw more immediately successful, and not traceable to any obvious influence, English or foreign, came the comedies of Oscar Wilde. For a parallel to their pure delight and high spirits, and to the exquisite wit and artifice with which they were constructed, one would have to go back to the dramatists of the Restoration. To Congreve and his school, indeed, Wilde belongs rather than to any later period. With his own age he had little in common; he was without interest in its social and moral problems; when he approved of socialism it was because in a socialist state the artist might be absolved from the necessity of carrying a living, and be free to follow his art undisturbed. He loved to think of himself as symbolic, but all he symbolized was a fantasy of his own creating; his attitude to his age was decorative and withdrawn rather than representative, He was the licensed jeste. to society, and in that capacity he gave us his plays. Shaw may be said to have founded a school; at any rate he gave the start to Galsworthy and some lesser dramatists. Wilde founded nothing, and his works remain as complete and separate as those of the earlier artificial dramatists of two centuries before.

Another school of drama, homogeneous and quite apart from the rest, remains. We have seen how the "Celtic Revival," as the Irish literary movement has been called by its admirers, gave us a new kind of romantic poetry. As an offshoot from it there came into being some ten years ago an Irish school of drama, drawing its inspiration from two sources—the body of the old Irish legends and the highly individualized and richly-coloured life of the Irish peasants in the mountains of Wicklow and of the West, a life, so the dramatists believed, still unspoiled by the deepening influences of false system of education and the wear and tear of a civilization whose values are commercial and not spiritual or artistic. The school founded its own theatre, trained its own actors, fashioned its own modes of speech (the chief of which was a frank restoration of rhythm in the speaking of verse and of cadence in prose), and having all these things it produced a series of plays all directed to its special ends, and all composed and written with a special fidelity to country life as it has been preserved, or to what it conceived to be the spirit of Irish folk-legend. It reached its zenith quickly, and as far as the production of plays is concerned, it would seem to be already in its decline. That is to say, what in the beginning was a fresh and vivid inspiration caught direct from life has become a pattern whose colours and shape can be repeated or varied by lesser writers who take their teaching from the original discoverers. But in the course of its brief and striking course it produced one great dramatist—a writer whom already not three years after his death, men instinctively class with the masters of his art.

J.M. Synge, in the earlier years of his manhood, lived entirely abroad, leading the life of a wandering scholar from city to city and country to country till he was persuaded to give up the Continent and the criticism and imitation of French literature, to return to England, and to go and live on the Aran Islands. From that time till his death---some ten years—he spent a large part of each year amongst the peasantry of the desolate Atlantic coast and wrote and plays by which his name is known. His literary output was not large, but he supplied the Irish dramatic movement with exactly what it needed—a vivid contact with the realities of life. Not that he was a mere student or transcriber of manners. His wandering life among many peoples and his study of classical French and German literature had equipped him as perhaps no other modern dramatist has been equipped with an imaginative insight and a reach of perception which enabled him to give universality and depth to his portrayal of the peasant types around him. He got down to the great elemental forces which throb and pulse beneath and common crises of everyday life and laid them bare, not as ugly and horrible, but with a sense of their terror, their beauty and their strength. His earliest play, *The Well of the Saints*, treats of a sorrow that is as old as Helen of the vanishing of beauty and the irony of fulfilled desire. The great realities of death pass through the *Riders to the Sea*, till the language takes on a kind of simplicity as of written words shrivelling up in a flame. *The Playboy of the Western World* is a study of character, terrible in its clarity, but never losing the savour of imagination and of the astringency and saltness that was characteristic of his temper. He had at his command an instrument of incomparable fineness and range in the language which he fashioned out the speech of the common people amongst whom he lived. In his dramatic writing this language took on a kind of rhythm which had the effect of producing a certain remoteness of the highest possible artistic value. The people of his imagination appear a little disembodied. They talk with that straightforward and simple kind of innocency which makes strange and impressive the dialogue of Maeterlinck's earlier plays. Through it, as Yeats has said, he saw the subject-matter of his art "with wise,, clear-seeing, unreflecting eyes— and he preserved the innocence of good art in an age of reasons and purposes." He had no theory except of his art; no "ideas" and no problems"; he did not wish to change anything or to reform anything; but he saw all his people pass by as before a window, and he heard their words. This resolute refusal to be interested in or to take account of current modes of thought has been considered by some to detract from his eminence. Certainly if by "ideas" we mean current views on society or morality, he is deficient in them; only his very deficiency brings him nearer to the great masters of drama—to Ben Johnson, to Cervantes, to Moliere— even to Shakespeare himself. Probably in no single case amongst our contemporaries could a high and permanent place in literature be prophesied with more confidence than in his.

In the past it has seemed impossible for fiction and the drama, i.e. serious drama of high literary quality, to flourish, side by side. It seems as though the best creative minds in any age could find strength for any one of these two great outlets for the activity of the creative imagination. In the reign of Elizabeth the drama outshone fiction; in the reign of Victoria the novel crowded out the drama. There are sings that a literary era is commencing, in which the drama will again regain to the full its position as a literature. More and more the bigger creative artists will turn to a form which by its economy of means to ends, and the chance it gives not merely of observing but of creating and displaying character in action, has a more vigorous principle of life in it than its rival.

The very recent English literature has appeared in different styles having great creativeness.

In India also, Jawaharlal Nehru, Srinivasa Iyengar and Indira Gandhi as political speakers; Auropindo, Sarojini Naidu and Rabindranath Tagore as poets; and Mulk Raj Anand, R.K.Narayan, Raja Rao, etc., as novelists made a mark in the English literary world.

ENGLISH LANGUAGE

Language is a method of communicating ideas, feelings and or desires by means of a system of sound symbols. It aims at expression that is clear and expression that is free. English is a language followed by billions of people all over the world.

Pronunciation

The most important and practical aspect of language is to cultivate an ability of conversation which requires good pronunciation. Effective communication depends on the efficient use of a word and its internationally accepted pronunciation. So far as the English pronunciation is concerned, the standard could only be stated as being that of educated English-speaking people, though actually this might need a little qualifying (Gauntlet). In an ideal pronunciation, at any rate, what might be referred to as the non-significant element of speech must be present. Of course, it is not necessary for an ideal pronunciation to be markedly Southern British or markedly any other speech dialect. Many authors on English pronunciation, including Palmer, recommend a modified form of Southern British pronunciation. To acquire good pronunciation one must get adequate training in phonetics.

Phonetics

Phonetic notation is necessary for correct pronunciation. There will be a systematic phonetic notation in different scripts and adopt a new speech-basis, that is, the habit of using the organs of speech-lips, tongue, palate, teeth-ridge, etc. English spelling and pronunciation have no rational phonetic basis (Panchal, 1984). So the learners must learn what speech sounds are and how sounds are produced. They should add to the checking power of the ear, the construction power of placing the tongue in certain positions so as to produce correct sounds. The listening and imitation processes should be supported by the study of English phonetics. The knowledge of phonetics reduces the mistakes in pronunciation made by the users.

Spelling

Writing was purely phonetic in earlier days. Gradually individual differences crept into the pronunciation and custom and usage of writers, teachers and learned people fixed the spelling of English words. With the progress of time, spoken forms changed, but they continued to be written in the same original way. Books which could not check changes in pronunciation tended to stereotype spelling, and it was a pretty long time since speech and spelling have fallen out of harmony. One can speak English credibly but when he comes to write it, problems arises. Satisfactory rules for the guidance have not been found out simply because the spelling of modern English language is curiously irregular and inconsistent. Words like 'to', 'two' and 'too'; and 'seize', 'cease' and 'seas' are differently spelt, though their pronunciation is very much the same. And words like 'cut' and 'put'; 'come' and 'home'; and 'great' and 'cheat' are similar in spelling but are pronounced differently. Letters such as 'e' and 'gh' are unnecessarily used in words like 'night', 'fight', 'write' and 'white'. English spelling is freakish and is not amenable to any rules. So drill, dictation, perception, spelling games, etc., help to improve the knowledge of spelling.

Grammar

Language is the vehicle of our ideas and feelings and grammar is the machinery by which that vehicle is set and kept in motion, the motive power is the mind, the speech sounds are the air, and space through which the movement of the vehicle takes place. Language precedes grammar and that grammar is a means and not an end in itself. The users must be firmly grounded in the exercise of correct grammar if they are to attain any skill or effective use of the language.

Some of the English language areas are explained to a limited extent in order to leave a chance to the language learners to peep into the details of English language.

OBJECTIVES OF ENGLISH TEACHING

The desired outcome at which instruction is aimed is called an educational objective. During the last five or six decades several discussions, workships, conferences have been arranged all over the world to discuss about the objectives— of Science, Social Studies, Languages, etc. The concept of objective-based teaching and evaluation has been discussed and analyzed in detail in these workshops and meetings by experts and practising teachers. While stating the objectives they have also developed the specifications to each objective in terms of behavioural outcomes. The objectives and their specifications of English based on the Report of All India Workshop held at Mysore in 1965 are mentioned herewith.

1. Knowledge

The student acquires the knowledge of

(a) elements of knowledge,
(b) forms of writing,
(c) textual context

Specifications

The student recognises, recalls, compares, discriminates, identifies, locates errors, transforms, analyses, synthesises, and substitutes in respect of

(a) under elements of language are included
  (i) grammatical structures (noun, verb, adjective, adverb, pronoun, proposition, conjuction, articles, tenses, phrases, etc.)
  (ii) sentence patterns (forms and concord)
  (iii) vocubulary (synonyms, antonyms, derivatives)
  (iv) spelling
  (v) punctuation
(b) under forms of writing are included
  (i) precise-writing
  (ii) letter writing
  (iii) essay writing, etc.
(c) under textual contents the teacher tries to cover
  (i) authors
  (ii) topics
  (iii) events
  (iv) ideas
  (v) characters
  (vi) emotions and feelings

2. Understanding

The student understands simple English when spoken.

Specifications

(a) The student recognises sounds of English words and their sound units.

(b) He differentiates sounds, or recognises contrasts in sounds of English words and in the sounds of words of the mother-tongue.

(c) He grasps the meaning conveyed by these sounds.

(d) He recognises the purpose from stress and intonation in a sentence or idiom.

3. Speaking

The student speaks simple and correct English.

Specifications

(a) The student reproduces the sounds correctly.

(b) He uses proper stress and intonation.

(c) He uses appropriate vocabulary and structures.

(d) He speaks with reasonable speed.

(e) He speaks with appropriate pauses.

(f) He puts his ideas in a proper sequence.

4. Reading

The student reads simple English with comprehension.

Specifications

(a) The student locates key words and phrases in a passage.

(b) He locates significant details.

(c) He locates key sentences in a passage.

(d) He gives suitable title.

(e) He gives the central idea.

(f) He draws inferences and interprets ideas.

(g) He establishes relationships.

(h) He locates the sequence of events, ideas and facts.

(i) He shifts relevant ideas and grasps the substance.

(j) He discriminates between ideas and grasps the substance.

5. Writing

The student writes simple and correct English.

Specifications

(a) The student writes legibly and distinctly.

(b) He uses appropriate words, phrases and idioms.

(c) He uses correct structures.

(d) He uses a variety of sentence patterns.

(e) He spells the words correctly.

(f) He punctuates sentences correctly.

(g) He organises ideas into paragraphs.

(h) He presents ideas and thoughts coherently and logically.

(i) He makes proper use of connectives.

(j) He reports the ideas with proper introduction and without repetition.

6. Translation

The student translates from the mother-tongue into English and vice-versa.

Specifications

(a) The student understands the vocabulary and structures used in the passage as a whole.

(b) He substitutes parallel words, phrases, idioms, and structures in the language of translation.

(c) He adds words to make the idea clear.

(d) He splits the large structures into short and simple ones, if necessary.

(e) He joins sentences to improve expression.

(f) He maintains the sequence of ideas.

(g) He maintains the spirit of the passage.

7. Appreciation

The student appreciates simple poems.

Specifications

(a) The student reads a poem effectively, with proper pronunciation, rhythm and intonation.

(b) He grasps the theme of the poem.

(c) He makes image in his mind with the help of picture-words.

(d) He quotes parallel lines.

(e) He memorises poems.

(f) He locates words with specific meaning in the poem.

(g) He draws inferences about the poet.

8. **Interest**

The student develops interest in English

Specifications

(a) The student reads English news papers.

(b) He listens to the English broadcasts.

(c) He joins reading clubs.

(d) He reads English magazines.

(e) He contributes to English magazines.

(f) He participates in debates and dramatics.

(g) He recites poems.

This list of objectives and specifications is not at all an exhaustive one, but only an illustrative one. The English teachers can develop, modify or use certain specifications according to their content, class room conditions, educational experience, etc., and can organise the activities accordingly. The ultimate objective of English teaching learning should be the development of proper communicating skills in the students.

NEED OF THIS RESEARCH

The current status of English has turned a significant percentage of the world's population into part-time users or learners of English. The widespread need for English as a second language or a foreign language puts a considerable pressure on the educational resources of many countries to provide English knowledge. Problems relating to the teaching of English are discussed world over-which range from practical questions concerning curriculum, methodology and testing more theoretical questions concerning the nature of second and or foreign language learning and the role of cognitive and affective variables in the acquisition process.

English can be described as the 'Mother Tongue' or 'First Language' of over 45 percent of the population of 10 countries; ranked according to greatest percentage of speakers of English-United Kingdom, Ireland, Australia, New Zealand, Barbados, Jamaica, Thailand, the United States of America, Canada, and Guyana (Fishman et al., 1977). In English-speaking countries like these, English, however, is not spoken as an identical manner. Different varities or dialects of English exist, reflecting such factors as an individual's degree of education, ethnic group, social class, or geographical location. The variety of English that is recognised by speakers of English as being the correct way of speaking, that is used as the basis for written English, and that is the variety generally used to teach English to those learning it as a second or foreign language is referred to as Standard English (Richards, 1985).

In many countries a language that is not the mother tongue of the majority of the population may still function as an official language, that is, as the sole or major language of law, government, education, business, and the media. In coutries where English has these functions, it is usually referred to as a 'Second Language'. English is an official (and hence second) language in Botswana, Cameroon, Fiji, Gambia, Ghana, India, Lesecho, Liberia, Malawai, Malta, Mauritius, Namibia, Naurway, Nigeria, Philippines, Sierra Leone, Singapore, South Africa, Swaziland, Tangania, Tonga, Uganda, Western Samoa, Zambia and Zimbabwe (Richards, 1985). When English functions as a second language, it is often regarded by its users as a local rather than a foreign language (Richards, 1979). Consequently, it is spoken in ways that mark its local status, Thus the countries like India, Nigeria and Singapore people refer to their English as Indian English, Nigerian English and Singaporean English. These are legitimate varieties of English with a greater total number of users than the varieties of English spoken in Countries where English is considered a native language (Smith, 1981; Kach, 1982). They often serve as vehicles for the expression of literature and creative writing. In their written forms they are close to standard British or American English, but their spoken forms may be quite distinctive (Richards, 1985).

In countries where English is not an official language it may still have a significant role to play. It may be an important school subject or it may be necessary to pass an examination in English to enter a university; it may be the language of certain courses at a university or at least of a large percentage of the students' text books; it may be needed for people who work in tourism, business, and for some sections of the civil service. In countries, where English has these functions, such as China, Japan, France, Germany, Mexico, Israel—English is not regarded as a second language—English is described as a 'Foreign Language'. In EFL (English as a foreign language) countries, as they are sometimes called so, English is increasingly the first foreign language studied at school or college. Over 50 percent of the world's non-English-speaking foreign students study in English-speaking countries. This has led to a greater need for English to be taught at the higher levels of education in EFL countries.

Increasingly English is becoming the major international language of printed information. A great deal of the world's commercial, economic, scientific, or technological knowledge is written and published in English, though the writers may be Chinese, Indians, Japanese or Italians. Publication in English ensures the widest possible readership for new findings and ideas and English is also an important language for the dissemination of news around the world.

One must consider the function of English as a common language, or lingua franca, that is, a language that permits people who have no common language to communicate. As English is widely taught or used as a second or foreign language, Japanese and German businessmen who meet, for example, use English as their language: when Swedish tourists observe Italy, their travel language is English and when French tourists visit Russia, their hotel language is English. English is the language that the English-speaking world uses to communicate with the rest of the world. The pressure of some 300 million largely monolingual speakers of English in the economically and politically important English-speaking countries in the world today creates further reasons for others to learn English.

The importance of English can also be seen from the emphasis given by the Indian University Education Commission : "English, however, must continue to be studied. It is a language which is rich in literature-humanistic, scientific and technical. If, under sentimental urges, we should give up English, we would out ourselves off from the living stream of our growing knowledge. Unable to have access to this knowledge, our standards of scholarship would fast deteriorate and our participation in the world movements of thoughts would become negligible. Its effect would be disastrous for our practical life. A living nation must move with the times and must respond quickly to the challenge of surroundings. English is the only means of preventing our isolation from the world, and we will act unwisely, if we allow ourselves to be enveloped in the folds of a dark curtain."

Understanding the importance of English teaching and learning, the achievement of secondary school students in English was considered for a detailed study. The results of this study will help in finding out the remedial measures for the enormous failures in English subject.

STUDY OBJECTIVES

The objectives proposed for this research are —

1. To find out the level of achievement in English of secondary school pupils.
2. To compare the achievement in English of secondary school boys and girls.
3. To compare the achievement in English of pupils studying in private and government secondary schools.
4. To compare the achievement in English of pupils studying in rural and urban secondary schools.
5. To compare the achievement in English of pupils studying in Telugu medium and English medium secondary schools.
6. To compare the achievement in English of pupils studying in residential and non-residential secondary schools.

STUDY'S SCOPE AND LIMITATIONS

English teaching and learning are concerned with the language and literature aspects. These two aspects are included in the syllabus and hence the measurement gives due weightage to these two areas. This study gives importance to sex, locale of the school, type of management, medium of instruction and to residential and non-residential type of the secondary school. An intensive study has been undertaken to study the achievement in English of secondary school pupils.

2

RELATED LITERATURE

A good research study in any field of knowledge requires an adequate familiarity with the works which have already been done in the same area. A summary of the writings of recognized authorities and of previous research provides evidence that the research is familiar with what is already known and what is still unknown and untested. Since effective research is based upon past knowledge, this step helps to eliminate the duplication of what has been already done. It is a valuable guide to define the problem, to recognize its significance, to suggest promising data gathering devices, to appropriate study design, to identify sources of data, to make effective analysis and to arrive at fruitful conclusions.

Citing studies that show substantial agreement and those that seen to present conflicting conclusions helps to sharpen and define understanding of existing knowledge in the problem area, provides a background for the research project, and makes the reader aware of the status of the issue. Parading a long list of annotated studies relating to the problems is ineffective and inappropriate. Only those studies that are plainly relevant, competently executed, and clearly reported should be considered.

In searching related literature, the researcher should note certain important elements. They include 1. Reports of closely related studies that have bene investigated. 2. Design of the study, including procedures employed and data-gathering instruments used. 3. Populations that were sampled and sampling methods employed. 4. Variables that were defined, 5. Extraneous variables that could have affected the findings, 6. Faults that could have been avoided, and 7. Recommendations for further research.

Capitalizing on the reviews of expert researchers can be fruitful in providing helpful ideas and suggestions. While review articles that summarize related studies are useful, they do not provide a satisfactory substitute for an independent research. Even though the review of related literature is not a substitute for an independent work, it is one of the first steps in the research process. Hence this collection of literature about the importance and objectives of science/biology teaching and about related research studies.

English is the major problems to many students to get through the examinations. This may be due to many reasons and hence let us identify some of the correlates of English achievement'.

The English achievement level was associated with attitude towards English, personal adjustment, social adjustment and socio-economic status (Abraham, 1974).

The factors that played a vital role for learning English and failures in English were intelligence, English vocabulary, knowledge of grammar, comprehension, spelling, pronunciation, speed and legibility of handwriting, the status of English in the family, and the quality of the teacher (Jain, 1979).

For over-achievers in English, only linguistic disposition and general adjustment were needed to account for total variance (Abraham, 1974).

For under-achievers in English, group adjustment, socio-personal adjustment and scholastic disposition were found by Abraham 1974 to be the factors responsible for explaining total variance.

Menon (1980) has observed a high correlation between language efficiency and achievement in English.

The performance of boys was superior to that of the girls in all branches (Thakur, 1972) Video-assisted instruction helped boys to achieve in English more than girls (Karpagakumaravel, 1991). Contrary to this, Abraham, (1974) found a greater proportion of normal achievers in English among girls as a against boys

Under-achievement in English was more frequent in rural schools and over-achievement in urban schools (Abraham, 1974).

Over-achievers in English were proportionately more in private schools than in government schools (Abraham, 1974).

Video-assisted instruction was effective in gaining scores (Karpagakumaravel, 1992) in English, and this finding is an agreement with the findings of the studies of Mohammad and Nadia (1980), Chandra (1986), Durai Samy (1989) and Indirani (1989) but it is disagreement with Michael John (1979), Bobby (1979), Gower (1970), Gosh and Sampoornam (1982) and Dhanabaghyam (1989) who were not able to find any difference between CCTV based instruction and conventional instruction and with Barrington (1965), Shaw (1973) and Roy (1973) who reported insignificant and negative impact of CCTV teaching.

3

RESEARCH DESIGN

Research design decides the fate of any research proposal and its outcome. As such it is regarded as the heart of any research. Designing provides a picture for the whole study before starting of the work. It is, in a simple language, a plan of action. It is, therefore, desirable to have a methodically designed research plan. So, the following aspects of the research design have been discussed in detail.

The operational definitions of the different terms used, the various hypotheses that were framed for verification in the present study and the rationale of these hypotheses have bene discussed.

The sampling techniques selected, the reasons for selection of a particular sampling technique, and the selection of sample according to different variables have also been discussed in detail.

The selection of suitable tool for the collection of data, and the procedure followed in administering the tool to collect the data required for the present study have also been explained.

Before going into the details of the sample, sampling techniques, variables and hypotheses, it is worthwhile to discuss the operational definitions of the key terms used in the present study which will enlighten the characteristics involved in each term.

OPERATIONAL DEFINITIONS

The operational definitions of the important terms used in the present study are discussed and defined herewith.

English

English is one of the languages used by mankind for communication. A notable percentage of people globally use English in different styles in different situations and purposes. English is mother-tongue or first language of the people of U.K., Ireland, Australia, New Zealand, Barbados, Jamaica, Thailand, U.S.A., Canada, Guano, etc., official language or second language in countries like Boatswain, Corneroon, Fiji, Gambia, Ghana, India, Liberia, Malta, Mauritius, Namibia, Nigeria, Philippines, Singapore, South Africa, Uganda, Zambia, Zimbabwe, etc., and foreign language in nations such as China, Japan, France, Germany, Mexico, Israel, etc. Everywhere around the globe English serves as a communication medium between/among individuals/communities/nations.

English is learned as language and literature. The former includes spelling, phonetics, pronunciation, structure, grammar, etc., and the latter covers the prose, poetry drama, fiction and novel. The language learning is necessary to understand and communicate well and the literature is important to enjoy the beauty of structure, to appreciate the creative thought and to get interest in the language and literature.

Achievement

Achievement in an educational institution may be taken to mean any desirable learning that is observed in the student Since the word desirable implies a value judgement, it is obvious that a particular learning may be referred to as achievement or otherwise depending on whether it is considered desirable or not. Understood in this way, any behaviour that is learned may come within the scope of achievement Achievement, according to Smith (1969) and Spencer and Helmrich (1963), is the test-oriented behaviour that allows the individuals's performance to be evaluated according to some internally or externally imposed criterion, that involves the individual in competing with others, or that otherwise involves some standard of excellence.

Academic achievement is related to the acquisition of principles and generalisations and the capacity to perform efficiently, certain manipulations of objects, symbols and ideas. Assessment of academic performance has been largely confirmed to the evaluation in terms of information, knowledge, and understanding. It is universally accepted that the acquisition of factual data is not an end in itself, but an individual who has received education should show evidence of having understood them. But, for obvious reasons the examinations are largely confined to the measurement of the amount of information which the students have acquired.

Achievement in terms of subject matter is conventionally assessed in our educational enterprises by employing a system of marks or grades. It has been strongly argued that marks are necessary for effective teaching and learning. Marks are necessary, as observed by Trabue (1926), for classification, guidance, and evidence of effort. A Committee of Principals in California listed the purposes of marks as the indication of the degree of mastery of subject matter and the prediction of future success. Madsen (1930) points out that marks set goals and motivate students. Symonds (1927) listed among the purposes of marks the following-incitement of study, promotion of competition, determination of promotion, assistance in education and vocational guidance, awarding credits and honors. It is universally accepted that marks serve as the basis of classification and certification, motivation and measurement of educational performance which have to be followed and maintained.

The effectiveness of any educational system is gauged to the extent the students involved in the system achieve, whether it be in cognitive, conative or psychomotor domain. In general terms achievement refers to the scholastic or academic achievement on the student at the end of an educational programme. To maximize the achievement within a given setup is, therefore, the goal of every educationist. Research has come to our aid by looking into what variables-personal, home college, teacher, etc.-promote achievement and what are deterrents to it. It has been thus indicated that a good number of variables, such as personality characteristics of the learners, the socio-economic status from which they hail, the educational aspirations, the organizational climate of the institution, etc., to mention a few, influence achievement in varying degrees.

Heads of institutions, curriculum planers, teachers and others who are involved in the task of helping students to achieve better, would like to have a knowledge of the extent of the influence these correlates exert on achievement. Further, a synoptic view of the researches done would be of utmost importance to the educational researcher to enable him to explore greater depths in this, rather important area of achievement (Anand and Padma, 1989).

Behind these arguments is the assumption that the students will be benefited by attaining excellence in academic achievement. The people associated with the achievement of students will look into the flaws and merits of the achievement and take necessary steps to enhance the academic achievement.

Achievement Test

Freeman (1965) defines a test of educational achievement as a test 'designed to measure knowledge, understanding, skills in a specified subject or group of subjects'. Thus, according to Freeman, an educational achievement test measures an individual's knowledge, understanding and or skills in a particular branch of knowledge or some branches of knowledge. Further, Freeman is of the view that through educational achievement test, it is possible to ascertain how much does a person know after receiving education or training in a particular branch of knowledge.

The standardized achievement test is used to determine the degree of achievement in specific subject matter areas (Smith, Krouse and Atkinson, 1969). Achievement Test (Best, 1982) attempts to measure what an individual has learned - his or her present level of performance.

Anastasi (1961) has discussed the various uses of achievement test-achievement test is used to ascertain the attainment of minimum performance standards. In other words, achievement test is to find out whether an individual has attained the required ability in a given field of knowledge or activity. Another important use of achievement test is to be seen when there is a need for selecting candidates in regard to certain jobs or courses.

Achievement test is also used for purposes of guidance and counselling. It has been found useful in remedial teaching programmes as well as in determining the class to which pupil should be admitted. Administration of this test at regular intervals in helpful for the teachers is knowing the kinds of difficulties faced by pupils in learning. Finally it may be stated that the achievement test may be used as aid in the evaluation of teaching, the importance of instructional techniques, and the revision of curriculum content.

Private Schools

The schools managed by private organisations or persons, either partially or totally, were included in private schools. So, the public schools, Government recognized and aided schools managed by individuals or private agencies were included under private schools.

Government Schools

The schools under the sole management of Government were included under Government schools. So, the schools managed by Zilla Praja Parishads, Municipalities and Government were included in this category.

Urban Schools

The Schools located in an urban area were considered urban schools. An urban area should have a municipal corporation, cantonment board or notified town area committee etc.; should have a minimum population of five thousands; should have 75% of its male working population engaged in non-agricultural pursuits; and should have a population of at least 400 persons per square kilometer.

Rural Schools

The school located in rural area were considered rural schools. A rural area should have a population below five thousands, with 75% of its population engaged in agricultural pursuits.

Residential Schools

The pupils stay on the school premises with their teachers instead of coming from their houses daily. By this, the pupils spend all their time either on the school campus or in the hostels and pursue studies under the constant supervision of teachers. Such schools were considered residential schools.

Non-residential Schools

The pupils of these schools will be in the school campus only during instructional hours and spend their remaining time of home or at other places. Such schools were considered non-residential schools.

VARIABLES

The variables selected for the present study were (1) boys versus girls, (2) private versus government schools, (3) rural versus urban schools, (4) English versus Telugu medium schools, and (5) residential versus non-residential schools. The rationale for choosing the above stated variables is discussed herewith.

Boys versus Girls

In olden days, the boys were educated and the girls were restricted to their kitchens by their adult community. Times changed and the elders recognized the importance of women education. In the words of our late Prime Minister Pandit Jawaharlal Nehru, "If you educate a man you educate a person; if you educate a woman you educate the entire family". In the course of time woman's education gained importance and many parents are encouraging their daughters to pursue higher education. The women are also showing excellence in all fields. Their presence is felt almost in all fields. The physiological conditions, exposure to society, education and other aspects of girls and boys vary differently. The boys are exposed to the society to a larger extent, but the girls spend most of their time in going through books or helping their parents at home. It is also familiar that girls mature faster than boys at the early adolescent stage, both physically and mentally. The above factors will have their own impact on English achievement. So, a comparison between boys and girls will reveal if any difference exists in the achievement in English.

English Medium Schools *versus* Telugu Medium Schools

Usually people felt that there may not be much difference in achievement between the students of Telugu medium and English medium. But many studies in various fields proved that the pupils studying in their mother tongue score better as they understand anything without any hindrance. For those pupils who are studying in English medium there will be a communication gap or delay in understanding a phenomenon owing to language hindrance. So, there will be a difference between Telugu medium pupils and English medium pupils. Hence, this variable was considered to see what will be the difference between these two groups in the level of achievement in English.

Private Schools *versus* Government Schools

The reputation of private schools is generally better when compared with that of the government schools. The pupils are exposed to better conditions and better study atmosphere in private schools. If better facilities are not provided in private schools, the parents will question the authorities concerned immediately, because they pay higher fees for their children. The library facilities will play a major role in achievement in English The quality of teaching is also supposed to be better in private schools. The teachers take more interest in teaching in private schools as they are always either in the fear of losing their jobs or immediately being questioned by the management about the quality of their teaching. Since the standard of teaching is supposed to be different in private and government schools, the achievement in English will be different in these two types of schools. Thus, it is important to study the degree of difference in achievement in English in private and government schools.

Rural School *versus* Urban Schools

The urban schools are well equipped in many aspects when compared with the rural schools. The buildings. The libraries, the teaching staff, the educational atmosphere, the competitive spirit among the pupil, the amenities provided to pupils to pursue education, the exposure to fairs, exhibitions, workshops, etc., the student participation in teaching learning process, the use of audio-visual aids, etc., will always be better in urban school than in rural schools. These will play a commendable role in achievement in English. A comparison between rural and urban school pupils will bring out the difference in achievement in English, if there exists any.

Residential Schools *versus* Non-residential Schools

The residential schools are supposed to be in better position in all aspects when compared with non-residential schools. The pupils of the residential schools stay in the school itself without going home after the regular classroom teaching learning activities. They study under the supervision of their teachers all the time, and clear off their doubts immediately either in the classroom or during the study hours. Contrary to this, the pupils of the non-residential school stay outside the school, except for 5 or 6 hours, and spend their study at home, but they have to wait for quite a long time to clear them off. The delay in getting them cleared off sometimes leads to carelessness or frustration. This teaching learning aspect will definitely play an important role in achievement in English. The infrastructural, and the library facilities will also be better in residential schools. In Andhra Pradesh, residential schools were started offering the best education to the pupils by providing facilities conducive to the progress of each and every student. The intelligent pupils will always be in a better position, because they are not mixed up with lesser intelligent pupils, like in non-residential schools. Considering the above facts, the pupils of residential and non-residential type of schools were taken into consideration to study the level of achievement in English.

HYPOTHESES

Achievement refers to a tangible accomplishment or proficiency of performance in a subject as measured using a test.

Anyone is assessed and measured in terms of scores or achievement in a particular subject if one is thorough with the subject along with the required personality characteristics, he will be in a good position to show better achievement in the subject concerned.

The achievement depends mainly on intelligence and aptitude. The other factors that appear to be associated with achievement are intellectual curiosity, ability to apply knowledge to new situations, memory, insight into the subject, positive attitude toward the subject, interest in the subject, skills in learning, conducive teaching learning atmosphere, and so on. It is of utmost importance to provide conducive atmosphere to the pupils for better achievement. This better achievement leads to further achievement in pursuit of higher education levels.

The following hypotheses have been formulated for this study for verification.

Hypothesis 1.

The secondary school pupils will possess high achievement in English.

Hypothesis 2

There will be a significant difference in English achievement in boys and girls of secondary schools.

Hypothesis 3

There will be a significant difference in English achievement in the pupils of private and government secondary schools.

Hypothesis 4

There will be a significant difference in English achievement in the pupils of rural and urban secondary schools.

Hypothesis 5

There will be a significant difference in English achievement in the pupils of Telugu and English medium secondary schools

Hypothesis 6

There will be a significant difference in English achievement in the pupils of residential and non-residential secondary school.

SAMPLE SELECTION

Consideration was given to whether the entire population is to be made the subject for data collection or a particular group is to be selected as representative of the whole population. The 'entire population' here refers to all the tenth class students of the secondary schools of Guntur district of Andhra Pradesh.

Of the two techniques, the second one namely, the selection of a group as a representative of the whole population was identified as more convenient and suitable. This technique leads to a considerable saving of time, effort and finance. As this sampling technique has many advantages, it was selected for the collection of data.

In any social research, various methods are used for selection and drawing of samples. After a detailed study of all these methods, and considering the variables selected for the research work, the stratified sampling method was considered most suitable.

In the stratified sampling method, the entire population is divided into smaller homogeneous groups (Best, 1982) or strata, and then the sample is selected within each group. Every sampling unit in the population is placed in one of the strata prior to the selection of the sample so that the sum of the strata is identical with the population.

Stratified sampling method has certain special merits and advantages as a technique of sampling. Auckoff, in this context, has rightly said that 'stratified sampling enables the researcher to make a comparison of properties of the strata as well as to estimate population characteristics' (Kerlinger, 1964).

In the stratified sampling method, the investigator will have greater control over the selection of the sample when compared with random sampling. In random sampling, although every group has a chance of being selected and included in the sample, there is every possibility, and sometimes it does happen, that certain important groups are left unrepresented. But, in stratified sampling method no important group is likely to be left out.

Stratified sampling method is the ideal one when comparison between different variables has to be made. For example, if comparison has to be made between private and government school pupils or between rural and urban pupils, it would be very difficult to select the required number of units through any other method of sampling. If any other method is used, the problem of bias and prejudice creeps in.

Replacement of units is also possible in the stratified sampling method. Normally if a particular unit is not accessible for a study, it is difficult to replace it by another, but in this method it is possible. Stephen stated that 'stratification automatically brings about a replacement of persons lost to the sample, by persons of the same stratum, thus partly correcting the bias that would result if there were no replacement of loses' (Festinger and Daniel, 1976). As the entire population is divided into particular strata it is easy and convenient to replace on inaccessible case by an accessible one.

Stratification process is an important aspect in the stratified sampling method. The following precautions were taken while stratifying the population: the variables involved in the study were taken note of; care was taken to see that each stratum in the universe was large enough in size so that selection of items could be done on random basis; the strata formed were definite and clear cut; each stratum was free from influence of the other; that there was no overlapping.

Certain fundamental principles were considered to make the sample scientific and clear-cut before actually selecting the sample.

Firstly, the 'universe' must be clearly defined. In the technical phraseology of research, the whole population out of which the samples are to be selected is known as the 'universe'. For the present research work, the universe includes all the students of tenth class studying in secondary schools of Guntur District of Andhra Pradesh. The study was limited to a particular geographical area to facilitate appropriate sample selection and to avoid bias and prejudice.

Secondly, decision has to be made about the units of the sample. A unit of sample may be a house, a family, a group of individuals or a single individual. A good unit should possess the following characteristics—1. **Clarity:** The unit should be clearly defined in unambiguous terms. This would make the study easy and efficient. For the present research work, a sampling unit was a pupil of tenth class studying in any school of Guntur district; 2. **Suitability:** a good unit should be well suited to the problem under study. Since the problem is concerned with the achievement in biology of tenth class pupils of Guntur district, the unit selected is well suited to the problem; 3. **Accessibility:** The unit selected should be easily accessible to the researcher. If the units selected are difficult to reach and if we fail to make use of them, the study would be vitiated. The selected sampling unit i.e., a tenth class pupil is easily accessible since he/she could be approached in any secondary school.

Thirdly, a source list must be obtained or prepared. A source list is the list which contains the names of the units of the universe from which the sample may be selected. It may exist even before the beginning of the project or it may be prepared afresh by the investigator himself. A source list was prepared consulting the district education authorities to select the sample.

Besides considering these principles, it is extremely important to think about the size of the sample to be selected. If the sample is either too small or too large, it will make the study difficult and also make the results untenable. According to Parten, on optimum sample in a survey is one which fulfills the requirements of effective representativeness, reliability and flexibility'. The size of the sample for the present research work was decided after considering the following factors.

Since an intensive study was planned, a very large number of sample were not selected. In case of an intensive study, very large number of samples are not so useful as they involve huge consumption or the resources. Hence, a reasonably smaller sample was found convenient.

The size and selection of the sample will also be influenced by the nature of the universe. If the universe is homogeneous, even a small-sized sample may yield dependable and required results. If the universe is heterogeneous, small-sized samples will not be useful. In case of the present study, the heterogeneous universe was split into smaller homogeneous strata and the samples were selected from these strata. For example, all the tenth class pupils of Guntur District were broadly grouped under rural and urban pupils. A required number of sample was selected from each of these two groups.

The investigator needs to determine the number of the groups to be formed. In case the number of groups proposed is large, the size of the samples shall have to be large so that every group should be of proper size and suit to the requirements of the study. In case the number of groups proposed is small, even small-sized samples can fulfil the requirement. In the case of the present study, the number of groups into which the universe was divided are-girls and boys, private and government schools, rural and urban schools, English medium and Telugu medium schools, and residential and non-residential schools. Since the number of groups are more, a reasonably large sample was to be selected from each of these groups.

Practical considerations and accuracy also play a vital role in determining the size of the sample. Every study is guided by certain practical considerations such as time, resources, accessibility of the data, etc. Generally, it is believed that a large-sized sample generally produces accurate results. This, of course, depends upon the sampling technique used. If the sampling technique is scientific, even small-sized samples can produce dependable and accurate results. While selecting the size of the sample for the present study, practical considerations like the availability of resources and time were taken into consideration. Care was taken to make the sample selection technique as scientific as possible.

The size of the sample is also governed by the size of the tools to be used. In case the tools are short, and the questions asked pertain to certain limited factors, a large sample can be selected. In case the tools are large and the questions complicated, the sample should be small in size so that, from administrative point of view, the investigator may not be put to unnecessary troubles. In the present study, a reasonably large sample was selected as the investigator used the marks of the sample.

The sampling method also determines the size of the sample. When random sampling method is used, the samples have to be large. On the other hand, if samples are selected through stratified sampling method, the reliability can be achieved even with the help of the small sized samples.

After taking into consideration all these factors which influence the size of the sample, it was decided that an ideal sample would consist of six hundred pupils. This sample is small enough to avoid unnecessary expenditure and large enough to avoid intolerable sampling errors.

Taking the variable which compares rural and urban areas at first instance, the Universe which geographically consisted of Guntur District was split into rural and urban areas. An equal number of sample was taken from both rural and urban areas, *i.e.*, 300 from rural and 300 from urban secondary schools.

The sample from the rural areas had to be selected from the tenth class pupils of Zilla Praja Parishad high schools, private High Schools and Andhra Pradesh Residential Schools. The two A.P. Residential Schools, one meant for boys and another for girls, were taken into consideration to get the sample for the comparative study of residential and non-residential system: sixty tenth class pupils were taken from each of these residential schools. To select the sample from the private high schools and Zilla Praja Parishad high schools of the rural areas, the lottery method as suggested by Best is used. In this method the names of all private high schools were written on slips of equal size, the slips were folded round, mixed well and kept in a container. It was decided to select 3 schools from private schools. So three paper slips were picked up from the container and the schools were thus chosen for sampling. Thirty tenth class pupils were taken as sample from each of the three private high schools giving equal importance to both boys and girls. The very same lottery method was followed in the case of the 3 Zilla Praja Parishad high schools. Thirty tenth class pupils from each school were taken as sample giving equal importance to both boys and girls.

Thus, a total sample of 300 were chosen from rural schools. Out of these, 150 were boys and 150 were girls; 90 were from private high schools and 210 were from government high schools; 120 were from residential schools and 180 were from non-residential schools; and all the sample were of Telugu medium.

Guntur, Tenali, and Mangalagiri towns were chosen as the urban areas for the selection of samples. A source list of all high schools present in these three towns was prepared. After the preparation of the source list of high schools, as all the schools were non-residential, the schools were divided into government and private schools. Further these schools were divided into Telugu medium and English medium schools.

The government schools selected were less when compared to private schools in urban area, but equal number of government Telugu medium and private Telugu medium schools of urban area were taken for the present study. As there were no English medium schools in rural areas, four English medium schools were selected only from the urban areas to collect the sample in order to make the sample equal in rural and urban schools. i.e., rural sample 300 and urban sample 300; and to make the equal sample of boys and girls from urban area. i.e., boys sample 150 and girls sample 150; and for equal sample of boys and girls out of total sample i.e., boys sample 300 and girls sample 300, the urban schools were selected accordingly. The total sample of 120 pupils of English medium were selected from the private schools as there were no English medium schools under the management of government in the district.

For selecting the different categories of schools of urban areas, the lottery method as explained in the case of rural sampling was applied.

Table 1 : Sample Distribution in Rural Schools

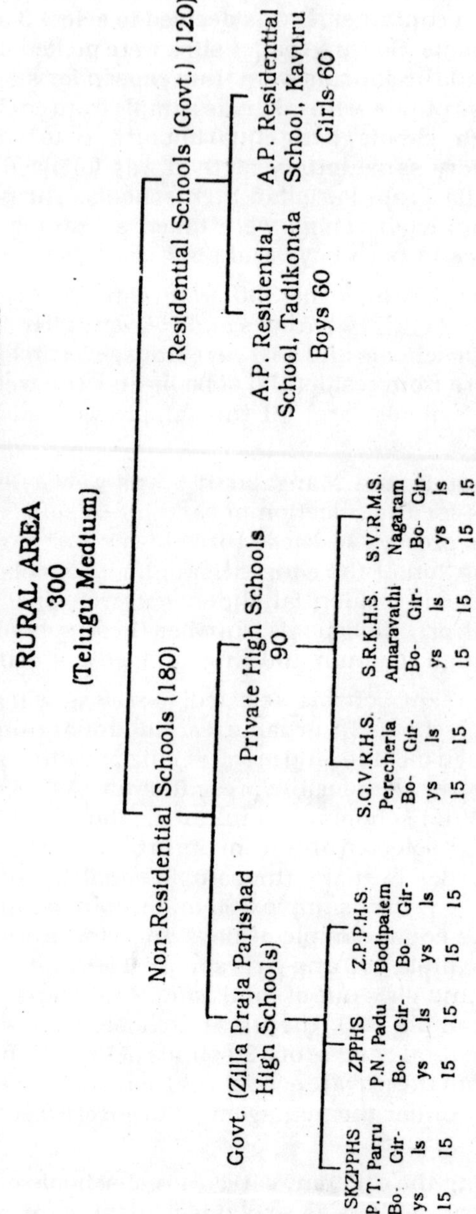

Table 2 : Sample Distribution in Urban Schools

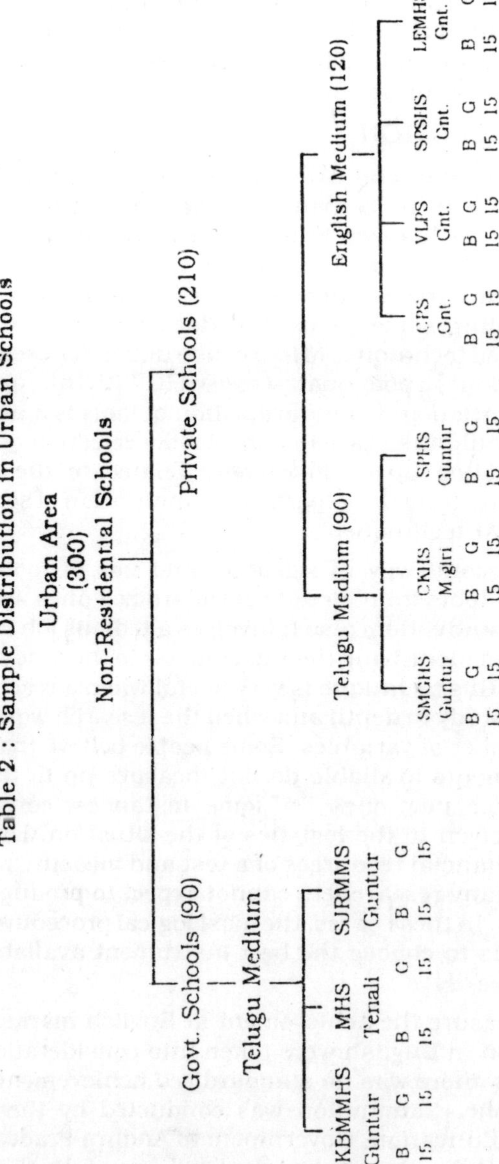

The total sample includes- Rural Schools- 300 and Urban Schools-300; Government Schools-300 and Private Schools - 300; Girls - 300 and Boys - 300; Residential Schools - 120 and Non-Residential Schools- 480; and English medium- 120 and Telugu medium - 480. The total sample was 600 tenth class pupils studying in Secondary Schools.

DATA COLLECTION

The selection and use of tools can be done in two ways. The first one is to construct a tool independently by the investigator for his own study. On construction of their own tools. Anand and Padma felt that 'a note of caution has to be struck when a researcher develops a tool for his study by merely pooling some items and does not subject it to the sophisticated techniques of tool construction. The result would be then obvious, a poor quality research. With this, one can say that preparation and standardization of tools is a major task, and one should take care in aspects like selection of area and sample, pooling up of statements related to the area and sample, consulting the experts, and application of sophisticated statistical techniques'.

The second way of selection and use of tools is right selection of tools from already standardized ones available in the field of study. Here also it involves a tedious job in locating the tools and identifying their usefulness to the study on hand. Even then, this technique is very useful when a research work is taken to study in depth and when the research work involves a good number of variables. Some people believe that some of the instruments available do not measure up to their standards. Hence new ones. In some instances, consideration should be given to the logistics of the situation. Locking the time and financial resources of a test and measurement organization, many researchers cannot expect to produce a better instrument. In these cases, the most logical procedure that one can follow is to choose the best instrument available for his purpose (Pearl).

To measure the achievement in English marks of public examination in English were taken into consideration. It was done so, 'as there was no standardized achievement test and as the public examination was conducted by the Board of Secondary Education, Government of Andhra Pradesh. Under these conditions, the marks taken will serve fully the research purpose.

DATA ANALYSIS AND FINDINGS

The mass data collected need to be systematized and organized, i.e., edited, classified and tabulated before it can serve the purpose. Here, editing implies the checking of gathered data for accuracy, utility and completeness; classifying refers to the dividing of the information into different categories, classes or heads, for use; and tabulating denotes the recording of the classified material in accurate mathematical terms, e.g., marking and counting frequency tallies for different items on which information is gathered. The analysis of the data was carried out in the following way.

The total score of English examination in the public examination of tenth class was taken to measure the level of achievement the maximum score that a pupil can get was 100 and the minimum score was 1. In the present study, the highest score secured by a pupil was 87 and the lowest was 12.

For the purpose of classification of categories of achievement, class system was applied. The pupil who scored 50 and below was kept in low achievement (fail or 3rd class) group, the pupil who scored between 51 and 60 was kept in average achievement (second class) group, and the pupil who scored 61 and above was kept in high achievement (first class or distinction) group.

Hypothesis 1 : The secondary school pupils will possess high achievement in English.

To test the validity of hypothesis 1, the following computations were applied.

Table 3: Level of English achievement in whole sample

Sample	*Mean*	*Standard Deviation*
600	48.6	22.7

The mean score status that the pupils were with low achievement in English. As per the standard deviation, the marks in the sample were dispersed to a high degree.

The scores of the units, further, were used to identify the level of distribution of English achievement in the whole sample.

Table 4: Distribution of English achievement in whole sample

Sample		*Low*	*Average*	*High*
600	f_o	287	255	58
	f_e	96	408	96

f_o = frequency of occurrence of observed facts
f_e = frequency of occurence expected on some hypothesis

As per distribution values, it can be said that the English achievement was not normally distributed. The concentration of achievement was tending towards low category.

The hypothesis 'that the secondary school pupils will possess high achievement in English' can be rejected as the sample possessed a low achievement in English.

Hypothesis 2 : There will be a significant difference in English achievement in boys and girls of secondary schools.

A comparison was made between boys and girls to identify the difference in English achievement.

There was a significant difference in English achievement between boys and girls. Boys were with average achievement, where as girls were possessing low achievement in English.

Table 5 : Comparison of English achievement in boys and girls

Variable	*Sample*	*Mean*	*Mean Difference*
Boys	300	56.3	15.4
Girls	300	40.9	

It was further tried to identify the level of distribution of English achievement in boys and girls.

Table 6: Distribution of English achievement in boys and girls

Variable	*Sample*		*Low*	*Average*	*High*
Boys	300	f_o	110	141	49
		f_e	48	204	48
Girls	300	f_o	180	109	11
		f_e	48	204	48

The distribution of English achievement in boys and girls was not normal. Its trend was towards average achievement in boys and towards low achievement in girls.

The hypothesis that 'there will be a significant difference in English achievement in boys and girls' can be accepted as there was a difference.

Hypothesis 3 : There will be a significant difference in English achievement in the pupils of private and government secondary schools

A comparison, to test the validity of the hypothesis, was made between private and government schools.

Table 7 : Comparison of English achievement in the pupils of private and government schools

Variable	*Sample*	*Mean*	*Mean Difference*
Private	300	52.6	8.0
Government	300	44.6	

It seems clear that there was a significant difference in the level of English achievement in the pupils studying in private and government secondary schools.

It was tried to identify the distribution of English achievement in the pupils of private and government schools.

Table 8 : Distribution of English achievement in the pupils of Private and Government schools

Variable	*Sample*		*Low*	*Average*	*High*
Private	300	f_o	73	159	68
		f_e	48	204	48
Government	300	f_o	166	121	13
		f_e	48	204	48

The distribution of English achievement in the sub-samples was not normal. The achievement concentration was high in average category in care of private schools and it was high in low category in care of government schools.

The hypothesis that 'there will be a significant difference in English achievement in the pupils of private and government secondary schools' can be accepted as there was a difference.

Hypothesis 4 : There will be a significant difference in English achievement in the pupils of urban and rural secondary schools.

To test the validity of the hypothesis, a comparison was made between the achievement of urban and rural secondary school pupils.

Table 9 : Comparison of English achievement in the pupils of Urban and Rural secondary schools

Variable	*Sample*	*Mean*	*Mean Difference*
Urban	300	54.4	11.6
Rural	300	42.8	

There was a significant difference in English achievement in the pupils of urban and rural secondary schools. The achievement in rural pupils was of less category. The urban pupils were possessing average achievement.

Further calculations were attended to know the distribution of English achievement in urban and rural secondary school pupils.

Table 10 : Distribution of English achievement in the pupils of Urban and Rural Secondary Schools

Variable	*Sample*		*Low*	*Average*	*High*
Urban	300	f_o	111	168	21
		f_e	48	204	48
Rural	300	f_o	163	129	8
		f_e	48	204	48

The achievement in English was not normally distributed in both the sub-samples. The achievement concentration was in average category in case of urban pupils and it was in low category in case of rural secondary school pupils.

The hypothesis that 'there will be a significant difference in English achievement in the pupils of urban and rural secondary schools' can be accepted as there was a difference.

Hypothesis 5 : There will be a significant difference in English achievement in the pupils of Telugu and in the English medium secondary schools

A comparison was made to find out whether there exists any difference in English achievement in the pupils studying in Telugu medium and English medium schools.

Table 11 : Comparison of English achievement in the pupils of English and Telugu medium secondary schools

Variable	*Sample*	*Mean*	*Mean Difference*
Telugu	480	46.5	10.5
English	120	57.0	

There was a difference in English achievement in pupils of Telugu and English medium schools. The English medium pupils showed a high average achievement, but the Telugu medium pupils were with low achievement in English.

The distribution of scores of the pupils in various achievement groups was tested as below.

Table 12 : Distribution of English achievement in the pupils of Telugu and English medium Secondary Schools

Variable	*Sample*		*Low*	*Average*	*High*
Telugu	480	f_o	182	214	84
		f_e	76.8	326.4	76.8
English	120	f_o	9	97	14
		f_e	19.2	81.6	19.2

The English achievement was distributed without much difference. The achievement concentration in both the sub-samples was in average category.

The hypothesis that 'there will be a significant difference in English achievement in the pupils of Telugu and English medium secondary schools' can be accepted as there was a difference.

Hypothesis 6 : There will be a significant difference in English achievement in the pupils of non-residential secondary schools.

The following calculations were made to identify the difference between the two sub-samples.

Table 13 : Comparison of English achievement in the pupils of residential and non-residential secondary schools

Variable	*Sample*	*Mean*	*Mean Difference*
Residential	120	61.1	15.6
Non-Residential	480	45.5	

There was a significant difference in the level of English achievement in the pupils of residential and non-residential schools. Residential pupils were superior than non-residential pupils by possessing high achievement in English. The non-residential school pupils were with low achievement.

The distribution of achievement in the sub-samples was also tested.

Table 14 : Distribution of English achievement in the pupils of residential and non-residential Secondary Schools

Variable	*Sample*		*Low*	*Average*	*High*
Residential	120	f_o	5	41	74
		f_e	19.2	81.6	19.2
English	480	f_o	308	151	21
		f_e	76.8	326.4	76.8

The achievement distribution in residential pupils was towards high achievement category and it was towards low category in non-residential schools pupils.

The hypothesis that 'there will be a significant difference in English achievement in the pupils of residential and non-residential secondary schools' can be accepted as there was a difference.

The above results have given a clear picture of English achievement at secondary school level and they will help us in guiding and counselling our pupils to achieve well in English.

5

SUMMARY, CONCLUSIONS AND DISCUSSION

We don't know too much about the language (L. lingua= tongue) we speak everyday for our lives. Most of us, it is true, can get along fairly well without knowing very much about our own language and without ever taking the trouble to open a dictionary. But knowledge is power. The power of rightly chosen words is very great, whether those words are intended to inform, to entertain, or to move. English, one of the languages of mankind, is rapidly becoming a cosmopolitan means of communication and it is now studied by numerous people around the globe.

English is a Germanic language spoken originally in Britain but now spread to may parts of the world. It is the world's most widely known and used language. Its history may be divided into three periods. In the 'Old English' period (450 B.C.-1100 A.D.) four dialects were spoken: Northumbrian, Mercian, Kentish, and West Saxon. The last became the standard form at this item as many translations of Latin works were made at Winchester during the reign of Alfred the Great. 'Middle English' period (1100-1500 A.D.) includes five dialects, viz., Northern (developed from Northumbrian), West and East Midlands (diverging from Mercian), South Western (from West Saxon), and South Eastern (from Kentish). Each developed in characteristic ways but in general the influence of French after the Normal conquest brought new vocabulary and sound patterns. 'Modern English' (from 1500 A.D till date) was much influenced by the speech of London. English slowly became a relatively uninflected language with great flexibility in the way words may function. Its vocabulary is bout half Germanic and half Romance with many other borrowings.

The earliest works of the Old English were heroic poems, notably the epic 'Beowulf', which belong to a Germanic oral tradition of alternative unrhymed verse and were not put into written form until the seventeenth century. There were also a number of remarkable shorter poems, such as the elegies 'The wonderer' and 'The Seafarer', and many poems on Christian subjects. Major Old English religious writers, such as Bede and Alcuin, wrote in Latin; English prose started with the translations from Latin made by King Alfred and developed in the 'Anglo-Saxon Chronicle', the compilation of which he initiated.

Norman-French displaced Old English as the dominant written language after the conquest, but the native language, enriched by French, was firmly re-established in the fourteenth century in the Middle English poetry of Chaucer, whose works were indebted to Italian Renaissance authors, especially Dante, Petrarch, and Boccaccio. The native alternative tradition continued in such poems as 'Piers Plowman', 'Pearl', and 'Gawain and the Green Knight'. Printing was introduced in 1476 by Caxton, who published the culminating work of the Arthurian legend, Malory's 'Morte Arthur' (1485).

Although Chaucer had introduced Renaissance influences, it was not until the sixteenth century that the full efforts of humanism were felt, especially under Elizabeth I and James I, whose reigns mark the golden age of poetry and drama. The sonnet was introduced by Wyatt and Surry and polished by Sidney and others. Spencer produced the Elizabethan allegorical epic, 'The Faerie Queene', in 1590. The blank-verse plays of Kyd and Marlowe prepared the way for the dramas of Shakespeare, Johnson, and their seventeenth century successors. Donne and the Metaphysical School are the most important poets of the early seventeenth century, while Milton dominates the latter part. Among the most influential prose works were the anthorised versions of the Bible and Bunyan's 'The Pilgrim's Progress' of 1678.

During the restoration (from 1660), Dryden developed the heroic couplet in his satires and made an important contribution to Modern English prose in criticism. Drama, curbed during the Interregnum, was revived in the comedies of Congreve and Wycherley. The classical ideals of the Augustan Age (1690-1740 A.D.) were embodied in the satirical verse of Pope and the essays of Addison and Steele and were maintained by later writers, such as Johnson, Goldsmith, and Sheridan, Swift was the outstanding prose satirist of the period.

Various social and economic factors during the early eighteenth century contributed to the emergence of the novel, pioneered by Richardson, Fielding, Defoe, Smollett, Sterne, and various authors of the 'gothic' novel of horrors. It reached its full development in the works of Jane Austen, Walter Scott, Thakeray, the Brontes, Dickens, George Eliot, Trollope, Meredith, Hardy, Conrad, Bennett, and the American Henary James.

Classicism of the previous period was challenged in the early nineteenth century by the Romantic Movement. Its precursor was Blake and its leading figures were Wordsworth, Coleridge, Keats, Shelly, and Byron. Their Chief successors in the Victorian era were Tennyson, Browning, Mathew Arnold, and Surinburne. Macanlay, John Stuart Mill, Carlyle, Ruskin, and Pater were among the influential prose writers.

At the turn of the century the comedies of Wilde and Shaw enlivened the English theatre; prior to World War I Kipling, Hardy, Yeats, Belloc, Chesterson, Wells, Housman, and de la Mare produced a distinguished today of verse as well as fiction and criticism. The poets associated with the war period were Brooke, Owen, Sassoon and Graves. Post-war poetry was dominated by Eliot, Auden, MacNeice, Day Lewis, Spender, and the later work of yeats. Among the leading novelists and prose writers were Forster, Joyce, D.H. Lawrence, Woolf, Aldous Huxley, Orwell, Isherwood, Greene, and Evelyn Waugh. Between World War II and the present appeared the poems of Dylan Thomas, Philip Larkin, Ted Hughes, and Thom Gunn; the plays of Osborne, Wesker, Pinter, Beckett, Joe Orton, and Tom Stoppard; and the novels of Angus Wilson, Kingsley Attis, Muriel Spark, Iris Murdoch, Anthony Powell, and Antheny Burgess.

Rabindranth Tagore (Nobel laurete), Sarojini Naidu and Aurobindo as poets and R.K. Narayan, Mulk Raj Anand, Raja Rao, etc., as novelists from India have influenced the English literature to a great extent.

All languages have certain things in common, which include a sound pattern, words, and grammatical structure. 'A sound pattern' is a group of sounds that the human speech organs can utter; most languages have from 20 to 60 of these sounds. 'Words' are sounds or sound-patterns that have a meanings; words may stand for objects, actions, and or ideas. 'Grammatical structure' is the manner in which words are combined to form larger, meaningful units such as sentences. Grammatical structure may take either or both of the two forms- one form called syntax which is the arrangement of words in a particular order to make their meaning clear; and the other form called morphology uses a variation in the form of a word to show the function of the word in a group. Modern English uses a blend of syntax and morphology.

The present study, identifying the importance of English, has been taken up to achieve the following objectives.

Objectives were identified keeping the different aspects of the present study in view. The main objectives of the study were: 1. To find out the achievement of secondary school pupils in English 2. To compare the achievement in English of boys and girls, rural and urban schools, English and Telugu medium schools, private and government schools and residential and non-residential schools.

Considering their role in determining achievement in English, variables such as boys versus girls, rural versus urban schools. English versus Telugu medium schools. Private versus government schools, and residential versus non-residential schools were selected.

Hypotheses were formulated taking the above objectives into consideration. These hypotheses were formulated only in a positive manner. The main hypothesis of the present study was - The secondary school pupils will possess high achievement in English.

Stratified sampling technique was found the most appropriate technique for the present study as this study involved splitting of the sample into a good number of groups according to different variables. Through stratified sampling only it is possible to divide the sample into different groups and choose pupils from each of these groups. Random sampling technique was also employed to select pupils from each group.

A sample of 600 was found appropriate because the study involves due intensity and detail, a sample with more than 600 pupils would involve a lot of resources and, the more important one, time. Less than 600 pupils would also bring about problems of representativeness. Hence, 600 was considered appropriate number for the sample.

Only the pupils studying in tenth class in secondary schools of Guntur district, Andhra Pradesh were included in the sample. This decision was taken because English of tenth class decides their future education.

Out of the total sample, 300 pupils were from rural schools and 300 pupils were from urban schools. All the pupils selected from rural schools were of Telugu medium as there were no English medium schools in rural area. Regarding the type of school, 120 pupils were from residential schools and 180 were from non-residential schools. As regards to the management of schools. 210 pupils were from government schools and 90 were from private schools in rural area. An equal representation was given to both boys and girls in the rural sample. As regards to the schools in urban area, 180 pupils were selected from Telugu medium schools. Out of these 300 pupils, 90 were from government schools and 210 were from private schools. In this urban area also, equal proportion was given to both boys and girls. With the above splitting of the total sample into various strata, the final sub-group sample sizes were: boys- 300 and girls- 300, rural-300 and urban- 300, private schools -300 and government schools-300, Telugu medium -480 and English medium- 120, and residential schools - 120 and non-residential schools -480. Thus, the total sample (600) was split into different groups.

The marks scored in the public English examination of the tenth class were taken to assess the achievement of pupils. The results of the present study are:

"The achievement of secondary school pupils in English was low but it was nearer to average achievement category. Its achievement concentration was tending towards low achievement and the scores of the units were dispersed in the sample to a high degree."

. Research findings say that the English achievement level was associated with attitude towards English, personal adjustment, social adjustment and socio-economic status (Abraham);

the factors that played a vital robe for learning English and failures in English were intelligence, vocabulary, grammar, comprehension, spelling, pronunciation, hand-writing, the status of English in the learner's family, and the quality of the teacher (Jain); for over-achievers in English, only linguistic disposition and general adjustment were needed (Abraham); for under-achievement in English, group adjustment, socio-personal were the causes (Abraham); and a high correlation between language efficiency and achievement in English was observed (Menon).

Majority of the studies suggest to improve the grammar, vocabulary, spelling, phonetics, pronunciation, attitude of students towards English, efficiency of English teacher and home language environment besides the development of adjustment to various situations.

The English language teachers must consider these and they should try to improve all these language areas. They must also provide opportunities to read, speak, write, discuss, etc., besides becoming models to the students in and out of the classrooms. The students must be involved immensely in English literature and language by developing a positive attitude towards English, even when it is a second or foreign language. The language teachers must also equip themselves well in English language teaching as a first or second or foreign language.

"Boys were superior in English achievement than girls. They were with average achievement while the counter-parts were with low achievement. The achievement concentration was also in average category in boys and it was in low category in girls."

This result was in support of the study of Thakur in which the performance of boys was superior to that of girls and of the study of Karpagakumaravel in which the video-assisted instruction helped the boys to achieve in English more than girls; but it is against to the finding of Abraham where he found a greater proportion of normal achievers in English among girls as against boys.

We find in many cases no variation between the achievement of boys and girls, in the same manner a variation also in some cases. Whatever the achievement position of either sex may be, the English language teachers must try to enhance the achievement by meeting all the required language skills of each and every individual of the English class.

"The English achievement of the pupils of private schools was superior than government schools. The pupils of private schools were with average achievement and their counterparts were with low achievement. The achievement concentration of private school pupils was in average category and it was in low category in the other case."

This result was in support of the study of Abraham in which the over-achievers in English were proportionality more in private schools than in government schools.

The private schools are famous for their manual and material resources. The infrastructural facilities, the libraries, the teaching aids, the exposure to educational environment, the attendance, etc., will be superior in private schools. Moreover, the teachers have to work effectively in order to safeguard their personal as well institution's interests. In all, the instruction will be superior and it will help the students achieve better than their counterparts. These facilities are to be provided in government schools also to the most possible extent. There should also an effective supervision in government schools to make the teachers work to the satisfaction of the society. If same of these are followed, the government schools also come to fore-front in results as against to zero passes in some cases.

"The English achievement of the urban school pupils was better than the rural pupils. The urban school pupils were with average achievement while their opponents possessed a low achievement. The achievement concentration of urban pupils was in average category and it was in low category for rural pupils."

The finding of the present study was in support of another finding that the under-achievement in English was more frequent in rural schools and over-achievement in urban schools (Abraham).

In urban areas, majority of the schools are governed by private agencies which are famous for their efficient management. As the urban schools are managed by private agencies or individuals the schools will be with full equipment manual and material-which help in enhancing the achievement in English. These conditions and facilities should also be extended to rural schools to achieve on par with the urban schools.

"The English achievement of English medium secondary school pupils was superior than the pupils of Telugu medium schools. The English medium pupils were with high average achievement while the Telugu medium pupils were with low achievement. In both in sub-samples, the achievement concentration was relatively in average achievement category."

This result is not a strange one, but the English achievement of English medium pupils should be much more better than the present status. It seems that in both of the cases there is a mistake either in instruction or at learning point. The English teachers must try other methods than the existing ones-structural method, discussion method, translation method, oral presentation, etc. The students must involve immensely in language learning, otherwise it would be difficult to learn English language even to English medium students. The teacher must also give a detailed knowledge of grammar to the pupils.

"The English achievement of the pupils of residential secondary schools was far superior than the pupils of non-residential pupils. The achievement of residential pupils was of high category and it was of low category in non-residential pupils. The achievement concentration was also in high category in the case of residential pupils while it was in low category in the case of non-residential pupils."

This result is not also a surprising one because the pupils who get admission in A.P. Residential schools are the cream of the entrance test attendants. So there will be no surprise if they score excess than non-boarders. And at the same time we should not forget the manual material available round the clock to the residential pupils, the supervised study, the teacher pupil interaction the learning atmosphere, the competition among students, the exposure to reading, writing and speaking, etc., which play their rich role in learning and achieving well by residential pupils; which lack in case of non-residential pupils and which deserve the attention of pupils, parents and government. The possible and useful procedures from residential system can be applied in non residential schools.

On the whole it can be concluded that the "English achievement of the pupils of secondary schools was low. The boys, private school pupils, urban pupils, Telugu medium pupils and residential school pupils were superior than their counterparts. Only the residential pupils secured high achievement." The English must be taught by considering the individual needs and interests and by applying the latest English language teaching techniques. To enhance the academic achievement.

Suggestions for Further Research

The present study poses some problems to the future investigators in this field. They are—

1. Studies may be conducted on English achievement at various levels of education.
2. Studies may be conducted on the influence of independent variables on the dependent variables and vice versa.
3. Studies may be conducted on an experimental basis by using different types of English language teaching techniques to understand their relative efficiency in learning and achieving.
4. Studies may be carried out to find out the attitude of pupils and teachers towards English because it contributes much for learning and achieving.
5. Studies may be conducted on the influence of psycho-social variables on English achievement.

BIBLIOGRAPHY

Alpern, Moris L. (1946, October). "The Ability to Test hypotheses". *Science Education*. 30 : 220 - 229.

Anastasi, A. (1961). *Psychological Testing*. New Yark : MacMillan Co.

Aslam, Rekha (1992). *Aspects of language Teaching*. New Delhi: Northern Book House.

Barber, C.L. (1972). *The Story of Language*. London: Pan Books Ltd.

Barnard, Robert (1984). *A Short history of Englsih Literature*. New York: Basil Balckwell, Inc.

Best, John W. (1982). *Research in Education*, 4th ed. New Delhi: Prentice Hall of India Pvt. Ltd.

Bhaskara Rao, D. (1982). *An Evaluative Study of the New Science Curriculum at upper Primary Level In Andhra Pradesh*. Master of Education Disseration, Nagarjuna University.

Bhaskara Rao, D. (1982), June). "Education for Individual Responsibility". *Educational India*. 48: 185-187.

Bhaskara Rao, D. (1982, October). "An Evaluative Study of the New Science Curriculum at upper Primary Level in Andhra Pradesh". *Experiments in Education*. X: 147-149.

Bhaskara Rao, D. (1983, July), "Teacher : The Supreme of Mainkind". *Education*, 63: 193-196.

Bhaskara Rao, D. (1984, February). Private Educational Institutions". *The Educational Review*. XC: 34-36.

Bhaskara Rao, D. (1984), August). "Effective Communication in Teaching". *Experiments in Education*. XII : 119-111.

Bhaskara Rao, D. (1986, February). "Utilitsation of Community Resources in Science Teaching". *Junior Scientist*. 23 : 5-6.

Bhaskara Rao, D. (1987, October 10-12). "Science Education in Secondary Schools: A Reflection". *National Conference on New Education Policy - Its Need & Concept*. Department of Education, Hindu College. Mradabad, India.

Bhaskara Rao, D. (1998). *A Comparative Study of Scientific Attitude, Scientific Aptitude and Achievement in Biology at Secondary School Level*. Ph.D. Thesis, Osmania University.

Bhaskara Rao,D.(1989).*Dhrusya Sravana Bhodhapanakaranamulu* (Audio Visual Teaching Aids). Guntur: Nagarjuna Publishers.

Bhaskara Rao, D. (1989, October). "Objectives of Science". *Science Promoter*. 2: 701-703.

Bhaskara Rao, D. (1990, June). "Science Education in Secondary Schools". *Experiments in Education*. XVIII : 163-166.

Bhaskara Rao, D. (1991, September 16-18). "Biological Basis of Learning". Second International Conference on *Differentiated Psychology of Learning—Its Fundamentals and Application*, Martin Luther University, Halle, Germany.

Bhaskara Rao, D. (1992, August 2-8). "Teaching Learning Strategies in Environmental Education". *Eight Asian Symposium of the International Council of Associations for Science Education on Science Education for a Changing World*. International Council of Association for Science Education, Colombo, Sri Lanka.

Bhaskara Rao, D. (1992, July 8-14). "Quality or Equality". *Eighth Congress of World Council of Comparative Education Societies on Education, Democracy and Development*. charles University, Prague, Czechoslovakia.

Bhaskara Rao, D. (1992, May 11-15). "Scientific Attitude in Secondary School Pupils". *Second International Conference on History and Philosophy of Science and Science Teaching*. Queen's University, Kingstan, Ontario, Canada.

Bhaskara Rao, D. (1992, October 11-14). "Inderachievement: Identification, Diagnosis and Treatment". *Third European Conference of the European Council for High Ability on Competenc and Responsibility*. University of Munich, Munich, Germany.

Bhaskara Rao, D. (1993). *Vignanasasthra Bodhana* (Teaching of science). Guntur; Nagarjuna Publishers.

Bhaskara Rao, D. (1993, August 20-25). "Development of Educational Television in India." International Conference Teleteaching 93 on *Learning and Working Independent of Time and Distance*. Foundation for Continuing Education of the Norweigian Institute of Technilogy, Trondheim, Norway.

Bhaskara Rao, D. (1993, January 3-8). "Teacher's role in dealing with Learning Difficulties". *International Conference on Science Education in Developing Countries: From Theroy to Practive*. The Amos De-Shalit Israeli Science Teaching Centre, Jerusalem, Israel.

Bhaskara Ra, D. (1993, November 11-14). "Education for Peace - Need of the Day". Second Conference of the European Peace Research Association on *Improving European Security: Threats and Responsibilities*. Budapest, Hungary.

Bhaskara Rao, D. (1993, October 1-4). "Disarmament". Fifth International Castiglioncello Conference on *Conflicts and Disarmament*. Union of Scientists for Disarmament, Italy.

Bhaskara Rao, D. (1993, September 5-9). "Education vis-a-vis Democracy". Fourth School Year 2020 Conference The European Educational House IMTEC & COMED. Bogensee, Germany.

Bhaskara Rao, D. (1994). *Jeevasasthra Bodhana* (Teaching of Biology). Guntur: Creative Press.

Bhaskara Rao, D. (1994). *Scientific Aptitude*. New Delhi: Ashish Publishing House.

Bhaskara Rao, D. (1994, April 6-9). "Creativity and Academic Achievement". European Council for High Ability's International Workshop on *Creative Potential Exploring and Developing*. University degli studi di Pavia, Pavia, Italy.

Bhaskara Rao, D. (1994, October 8-11). "Special Activities for Talented in General Classes". Fourth Conference of the European Council for High Ability on *Nurturing Talent: Individual Needs and Social Ability*. University of Nijamegen, Nijmegen, The Netherlands.

Bhaskara Rao, D. and D.Pushpa Latha (1994). *Achievement in Biology*. New Delhi: Discovery Publishing House.

Bhaskara Rao, D. (1994, November 24-27). "Administrative Leadership in Educational Enterprises". The Fifth Annual Seminar of Educational Leadership International on *Educational Leadership and Social Changes*. Tallinn Pedagogical University, Tallinn, Estonia.

Bhaskara Rao (1995, July 30,-August 5). "Nonviolent Means to Combat Violence in Education". 1995 Congress of the International Education for Peace on *We the Peoples...... Educating for a World without Violence*. Norwich University Northfield, Vermont, U.S.A.

Bhaskara Rao, D. (1995, July 30-August 4). "enhancing Academic Achievement". The 11th World Conference on *Gifted and Talented Children-Maximizing Potential: Lengthening and Strengthening our Stride*, Hong Kong.

Bhaskara Rao, D. (1995). *Vidya Manovignana Sasthram* (Educational Psychology. Guntur: Creative Press.

Bhaskara Rao, D. (1995). *Animal Kingdom*. New Delhi: Discovery Publishing House.

Bhaskara Rao, D. (1995). *Batracology*. New Delhi: Discovery Publishing House.

Bhaskara Rao, D. (1995). *Scientific Attitude*. Ambala Cantt: The Associated Publishers.

Bhaskara Rao, D. and D. Pushpa latha (1995). *Achievement in Mathematics*. New Delhi: Discovery Publishing House.

Bhaskara Rao, D. and K. Vijaya (1995). *Achievement in Social Studies*. New Delhi: Discovery Publishing House.

Bhaskara Rao, D. and K. Vijaya (1995). *A Textbook Evaluation*. Ambala Cantt: The Associated Publishers.

Biswas, A. and J.C. Aggarwal (1987). *Encyclopaedic Dictionary and Directory of Education*, Vol. 1. New Delhi: The Academic Publishers (India).

Biswas, A. and S. Agrawal (1987). *Indian Educational Documents Since Independence*. New Delhi: The Academic Publishers (India).

Bloom, Benjamin S., ed. (1959). *Taxonomy of Educational Objectives, Hand Book 1: Cognitive Domain*. New York: Longman, Green and Co.

Bose, Kshanika (1992). *Teaching of English— A Modern Approach*. Delhi : Doaba House.

Brandwein, Paul F., Fletcher G. Watson and Paul E. Blackwood (1959). *A Book of Methods*. New York: Harcourt, Brace & World, Inc.

Bright, J. A. and G.P. McGregor (1970). *Teaching English as a Second Language*. Longman.

Buch, M.B., Chief editor (1987). *Third Survey of Research in Education*. New Delhi : National Council of Educational Research and Training.

Buch, M.B., ed. (1979). *Second Survey of Research in Education*. Baroda : Society for Educational Research and Development.

Burmester, Mary Alice (1953, March). "The Construction and Validation of a Test of measure some of the Inductive Aspects of Scientific Thinking". *Science Education*. 37 : 131-140

Bumett, R. Will (1960). *Teaching Science in the Secondary School*. New York : Holt, Rinehart and Winston.

Drabble, Margarett, ed. (1985). *The Oxford Companion of English Literature*. Oxford University Press.

English H.B. and A.C. English (1958). *A Comprehensive Dictionary of Psychoanalytical Terms*. London Longmans.

Evans, Ifor (1983). *A Short History of English Literature*. Middlesex : Penquin Books.

Festinger, Lean and Katz Daniel. (1976). *Research Methods in the Behavioural Science*. Amerind Publishing Co.

Fishman, J.A., R.L. Cooper and A.W. Conrad (1977). *The Spread of English*. Rowley, Mass : Newbury House.

Freeman, Frank S. (1965). *Theory and Practice of Psychological Testing*. 3rd ed. Calcutta: Oxford & IBH Publishing

Gage, N. L. (1966). *Handbook of Research on Teaching*. Chicago: Rand McNally & Co.

Garret, Henry E. (1979). *Statistics in Psychology and Education*. Bombay: Peffer and Simans Pvt. Ltd.

Haycraft, Brita (1984). *The Teaching of Pronunciation* — A Classroom Guide. Longman.

Karpagakumaravel (1991, July). "An Experimental Study on the Effectiveness of Video Assisted Instruction in Language Learning. *Journal of Educational Research and Extension* 28: 1, 23-33.

Mair, G.H. (1994). *Modern English Literature*. New Delhi : Discovery Publishing House.

Macmillan Encyclopedia, The (1981). London : Macmillan London Ltd.

Panchal, M.R. (1984). *Teaching of English*. Delhi : Vani Educational Books.

Potter, Simeon (1984). *Our Language*. Middlesex : Penguin Books.

Rathaiah, L. and D. Bhaskara Rao, (1995). *Achievement Correlates*. Ambala Cantt: The Associated Publications.

Richards, Jack C. (1985). *The Context of Language Teaching*. Combridge: Cambridge University Press.

Rivers, Wilga A. and Mary S. Temperely (1978). *A Practical Guide to the Teaching of English as a Second or Foreign Language*. New York : Oxford University Press.

Sharma, K. L. (1979). *Methods of Teaching English in India*. Agra : Lakshmi Narayan Agarwal.

Sood, S.C. (1988). *New Directions in English Language and Literature Teaching in India*. Delhi : Ajanta Publications.

Strevens, Peter (1977). *New Orientations in the Teaching of English*. Oxford University Press.

World Book Encyclopedia, The, vol. 12, L. (1992). London : World Book, Inc.

APPENDICES

ENGLISH - Paper I
(Third Language)

March/April 1994 **Parts 'A' & 'B'** Time:2½ Hours
Max. Marks: 50

Instructions:

1. *Answer the questions under Part A on a separate answer-book.*
2. *Write the answers to the questions under part B on the question paper itself.*
3. *Start answering questions as you read them.*

Part A (Marks : 20)
(Time: 1½ Hours)

Note : *Answer the questions under this part on a separate answer-book.*

(1-10) *Answer any five of the following questions in one or two sentences each:*

(5 × 2 = 10)

1. Why did the narrator try to 'look like a man with a quick temper'?

(My Financial Career)

2. The bright bangles are sings or 'tokens' of something. What are they tokens of?

(Bangle Sellers)

3. Why did the King send for his barber as soon as he discovered his horns?

(The King and the Tamarind Drum)

4. Why did Polya burst into tears on read into the letter from Maria Blokhina?

(Polya)

5. What are the methods Bahuguna used to persuade the children of Jardhargaon to protect trees?

(Chipko)

6. 'Sudha's amazing success story took an interesting turn...... What was the interesting turn it took?

(Dancing On)

7. Why was Gandhiji's meeting with Sardar Patel important?

(Death Before Prayers)

8. Lieutenant Blandford had asked Hollis Meynell for her photograph several times but she had refused. Why?

(A Test of True Love)

9. Why did Death drive his carriage slowly?

(Because I could not stop for Death)

10. 'I'm glad you made the mistake.....'. Why was the narrator happy that the young man had made the mistake?

(Christmas meeting)

11. Complete the following stanza:

Each for his own remembering, has a list
....
....
....
....
....
To me as music.

OR

If you were exchanged in the cradle and
....
....
....
....
but you are far away.

12. Read the following passage:

    We both sat down and looked at each other. I found no voice to speak.

    "You are one of Pinkerton's men, I presume," he said.

    (My Financial Career)

    Now answer these questions: (2×1=2)

    (a) Who are the 'we' referred to in the lines above?

    (b) Why was the narrator thought to be one of Pinkerton's men?

13. Read the following passage:

    'Blandford's attention was suddenly divided between the two. He felt a strong urge to follow the girl, yet he also had a deep longing for the woman.....

    (A Test of True Love)

    Now answer these questions: (3×1=3)

    (a) Who is the girl he wanted to follow?

    (b) Who is the woman he had a deep longing for?

    (c) Who had Blandford come to see?

Before you begin to answer, fill in your Roll No, and Centre of Examination.

Roll No........................Centre of Examination....................................

ENGLISH-Paper I

(Third Language)

March/April 1994 Parts 'A' &'B' Time:2½ Hours

Max. Marks: 50

Part B (Marks: 30)

(Time: 1 Hour)

Note : *Write the answers to the questions in this part on the. question paper itself.*

14. Complete the following passage using appropriate words. Each blank is numbered. Choose the correct answers from the four choices given. Put **a, b, c** or **d** in the blank. (5 × ½ = 2½)

Shravan is..............(1) orphan who came..............(2) Delhi from ....(3) Village.............. (4) Bihar. He worked in a tea shop in the village..............(5) a while before he left it.

1.	a) any	b) an	c) a	d) some
2.	a) to	b) from	c) by	d) in
3.	a) him	b) her	c) she	d) his
4.	a) at	b) on	c) in	d) to
5.	a) for	b) to	c) at	d) in

15. Match the parts of sentences under **A** with those in **B**. Write the letter of the sentence in B against the sentence in **A**. (5 × ½ = 2½)

A

1. Since it rained all day....... ( )
2. This bag belongs to him....... ( )
3. She hurt herself........ ( )
4. When I reached home....... ( )
5. She ought to know........ ( )

B

a) ....my mother had already left.

b)........that smoking is harmful to health.

c)........ we stayed indoors.

d)........while she was playing cricket.

e).......doesn't it?

16. Study the following pair of sentences and answer the question: (1)

    i) Satish held out a handkerchief.

    ii) Renu held a handkerchief.

    Who offered a handkerchief? Satish or Renu?

    Answer:..

17. Change the following sentence into passive: (1)

    They have recently built several dams.

    Several dams..

18. The thief saw the policeman. He then ran away. (Combine the sentences using 'when'.) (1)

    Answer:..

19. The music stopped. The child began to cry. (1) (Combine the sentences using 'as soon as'.)

    Answer:..

20. "I have seen this film twice," he said. (1)

    Answer : He said that...

    (Complete the sentence)

21. Fill in the blanks choosing the right words from those given in brackets. (4 × ½ = 2)

    (a) He was interested............painting. (in, at, to)

    (b) The magician turned the pieces of paper.............a bird, (to, into, of)

    (c) On hearing the news, show burst........tears, (at, by, into)

    (d) The building of the new road has been held ....due to bad weather. (over, up, by)

22. Choose the right words from those given in brackets and fill in the blanks: (4 × ½ = 2)

    (a) When they asked her a question, she........ to answer. (refused, rejected, denied)

    (b) I feel very........... in the company of strangers. (patient, uneasy, polite)

    (c) The little boy was afraid of his father. When his father called him, he went up to him rather............ .(softly, Stupidly, timidly)

    (d) I was.......... by the loud noise. (afraid, frightened, feared)

23. Fill in the blanks with words opposite in meaning to those italicized. (4 × ½ = 2)

    (a) Unlike his father who is a very *patient* man, he is generall_______________.

    (b) He is too young to know that is_________and what is *wrong*.

    (c) Treat him *gently*. Children of his age should not be dealt with_______________.

    (d) Although he is physically *strong*, he is_________, mentally.

24. Fill in each blank with the right form of the word in italics. (4 × ½ = 2)

    (a) He wants to leave *urgently*, but his principal doesn't seem to understand the______________.

    (b) The whole atmosphere in the village was filled with *smoke*. Most houses had dark and __________rooms.

    (c) To be_____________in life, stop worrying about *success*.

    (d) The more the police tried to solve the *mystery*, the more_____________it became.

25. Put the following words under correct headings :

    banking, colleague, nurse, architecture, nursing, architect, teaching, reporter. (8 × ¼ = 2)

Perseons	Professions
(a)...............................	....

(b)................................ ....

(c)................................ ....

(d)................................ ....

26. Complete the following using *ie, ei, ea* or *ee*. (2×½ =1)

(a) shr____ ____k

(b) st____ ____m

27. Complete the words with the letters given in brackets. (2×½ =1)

(a) respons______________ (able, ible)

(b) malic______________ (ious, ius)

28. One word in each list is spelt wrongly. Underline the wrongly spelt word. (2×½ =1)

(a) prestige, message, engage, hedge.

(b) special, social, offisial, unusual.

29. In the set of four words given below, the italicized parts in two words are pronounced in the same way. Find the words and copy them out. (2×½ =1)

(a) sponge, monkey, wrong, lone

(b) trousers, source, account, famous

30. Arrange the following words in alphabetical order :

seminar, seize, sentence, select (4×½ =2)

____________, ____________, ____________, ____________

31. Your friend is seriously ill. Advise him to take rest. (1)

....

....

32. What do the following sentences mean ? Put a [ ] mark against the right answer : (2 × ½ = 1)

(a) Can I leave now ?

(i) offering help [ ] (ii) asking for help [ ]

(iii) seeking permission [ ](iv) seeking advice [ ]

(b) Can I carry the bag for you ?

(i) offering help [ ] (ii) asking for help [ ]

(iii) seeking permission [ ](iv) seeking advice [ ]

33. Change the following into a polite request :

Ram to a stranger : I want to borrow your pen.

Answer : ....

34. Your teacher dropped his/her pen on the floor. You picked it up and gave it to him/her. He/she said 'Thank you'. What would you say to him/her ? Put a [ ] against your choice. (1)

(i) thank you [ ] (ii) that's all right [ ]

(iii) I'm happy [ ] (ii) that's my pleasure [ ]

ENGLISH - Paper II
(Third Language)

March/April 1994 **Parts 'A' & 'B'** Time:2½ Hours
Max. Marks: 50

<u>*Instructions:*</u>

1. *Answer the questions under Part A on a separate answer-book.*
2. *Write the answers to the questions under part B on the question paper itself.*
3. *Start answering questions as you read them.*

Part A (Marks : 20)
(Time: 1½ Hours)

Note : *Answer the questions under this part on a separate answer-book.*

(1-10) *Answer any five of the following questions. Each answer must be in a sentence or two :* (5 × 1 = 5)

1. "Bassanio went to his friend Antonio and told him of his problem". What was the problem ?
2. "I cannot trust his welth," said Shylock. Why could he not trust Antonio's wealth ?
3. What made Nerissa believe that the lottery of the caskets would bring Portia a good husband ?
4. Why was Portia unable to talk to Falconbridge ?
5. What did Shylock do when he learnt that his daughter had run away ?
6. What did the golden casket contain ?
7. Why was Antonio arrested and thrown into prison ?
8. How much money did Bassanio offer Shylock in the court? Why didn't Shylock accept it?
9. What gift did Bassanio offer the lawyer?
10. What good news did Portia bring for Antonio ?
11. Read the following passage carefully :

"You seem to be a worthy judge. Please go ahead and give

your judgement. No man on earth can change my mind. I will not accept anything except the pound of flesh that is due to me".

(The Merchant of Venice)

Now answer the following questions : (5 × 1 = 5)

(a) Who is speaking these words ?

(b) Who is the "worthy judge" being referred to here ?

(c) What does the speaker want ?

(d) "No man on earth can change my mind". How are the others trying to change his mind ?

(e) How is the pound of flesh due to him ?

12. Write a story using the hints given below in about 100—120 words. Divide the story into paragraphs.

a small grey mouse — old and wise — lives in large grey house — a black cat in the same house — mouse goes to kitchen — meets cat — cat happy — mouse agrees to go with cat for dinner — wants to put on red Sunday coat before going — cat agrees to wait — mouse runs into hole — never comes back.

OR

all animals of forest — decide to see who is beautiful — all happy — snake sad because she was ugly — cock kind — gives snake his crown — snake happy — moves like a queen — most beautiful — falls into a large pool — drops crown — looks for it — could not find — afraid to tell cock — cock waits for snake — calls again and again — snake never comes — cock gets up early morning and calls every day. (10)

13. Write a letter to your cousin explaining to him how you are planning to spend your holidays after the examinations.

OR

A shop in your locality has been playing music through loudspeakers causing great inconvenience to you and many others in the locality. Write a letter to the Sub-Inspector of Polic complaining about his. Add necessary details. (10)

Before you begin to answer, fill in your Roll No. and Centre of Examination.

Roll No.........................Centre of Examination.....................................

ENGLISH-Paper III

(Third Language)

March/April 1994 **Parts 'A' &'B'** Time:2½ Hours

Max. Marks: 50

Part B (Marks: 20)

(Time: 1 Hour)

Note : *Write the answers to the questions in this part on the question paper itself.*

14. Read the following passage carefully :

I have today become a cricketer, and all of you have heard of me, only because my uncle, Narayan Masurekar, noticed little things. It seems that Nan-kaka (as I call him) had come to see me in hospital the day I was born. He noticed a little hole near the top of my left earlobe. The next day he came again and took up the baby lying next to my mother. To his great surprise, he saw that the baby did not have the hole on the left earlobe. At once everyone started searching all over the hospital. I was at last found sleeping quietly next to a fisherwoman, not knowing anything of the trouble I had caused ! The mix-up had happened after the babies had been given their bath.

(The first Steps)

Now answer the following questions in a word or a phrase each : (5)

(a) When did Nan-kaka go to see the writer ?

....

(b) What did he notice in him ?

....

(c) Why was he surprised when he saw the baby the next day ?

....

(d) Where was the baby at last found ?

....

(e) When had the mix-up happened ?

....

15. Read the following passage carefully:

Some people were eating and drinking in a coffee house. A young woman was sitting alone at a table. She was wearing a beautiful diamond necklace. There was a tall, thin man at a table not far from her. He was looking at her necklace all the time.

Suddenly, the lights went out. The coffee house was in darkness. The woman started to shout. She was afraid. A few minutes later the lights came on again. The woman was in tears. She had lost her necklace !

The owner of the coffee house quickly shut all the doors. He telephoned the police. No one could get out of the coffee house. The police soon came. The police inspector told his men to search everywhere. They could not find the necklace.

The police inspector looked at the faces of all the people in the coffee house. He saw the tall, thin man and looked at him carefully. He went up to the man, picked up the bowl of soup that was on his table. He then poured to soup into a glass. The necklace fell out. The police caught the man and took him away. The young woman was happy to get her necklace back.

(a) Each of the following questions has three choices. Tick ( ) the right answer. (4 x 1=4)

1) The tall thin man was looking at her necklace because

i) it was beautiful,

ii) he wanted to steal it,

iii) he wanted to buy it.

2) When the lights went out the woman started to shout because

i) someone stole her neclace,

ii) she was afraid of darkness,

iii) she was alone.

3) The owner of the coffee house shut all the doors

i) not to allow the police to come in.

ii) not to allow the tall and thin man to get out of the coffee house.

iii) not to allow anyone to get out of the coffee house.

4) The tall thin man had hidden the necklace

i) under the bowl of soup.

ii) in the bowl of soup.

iii) in a glass of water.

(b) Given below are six statements. Three of them are true. Find the true statements and write (T) in the brackets. (3×1=3)

1) The young woman was sitting alone ( )

2) The tall thin man was sitting for away from her. ( )

3) When the lights came on, the woman was crying. ( )

4) The police came after the theft. ( )

5) The police inspector asked his men to search the tall, thin man. ( )

6) The police inspector had no suspicion on the tall, thin man. ( )

16. Read the following passage carefully :

Eskimos live in houses called igloos. An igloo is made of large square pieces of ice. But the igloo itself isn't square—it looks like half of a big white ball standing on a white field of ice.

It has a low opening for a door. It even has a window which is just a hole covered with a thin sheet of ice which lets the light in. An Eskimo can build an igloo for his family in an hour.

Inside this house, an Eskimo sleeps on a bed made of hard snow. He uses skins of animals for sheets and covers. There is always a lamp burning inside the house, which gives the light and is also used for cooking. The lamp is made of soapstone. It is filled with blubber, an oily material got from whales, which burns easily. Over the lamp is placed a cooking pot, also made of soapstone. Men, women and children wear clothing made of fur. When it is very cold, they wear two layers of fur clothing, one on top of the other. The first layer has the hair turned inwards and the second layer has the hair turned outwards. When it is warm, one layer of seal skin is enough.

Now answer the following questions : (2×1=2)

(a) The Eskimos depend on living beings on land and sea for two important things. What are they ? Answer in a phrase each.

1) ....

2) ....

(b) There are five words in List A. The meanings of four of them are given in List B. Choose the right word from List A to match each of the meanings in List B, and write it in the space provided against each meaning. (4× ½=2)

List A : field, sheet, fur, layer, warm

List B :

1) soft, thick find hair on some type of animals......
2) a covering that is spread on top of another thing........
3) an open area of land...........
4) a broad peice of something thin :............
5) not cold but not hot : ....

(c) Complete the following sentences using a word. (2×½=1)

i) Eskimos make igloos out of large pieces of........
ii) The Eskimo's...................is made of hard snow.

(d) An igloo is very different from the kind of houses most of us live in. However it is similar to our houses in two ways. What are they ? Your answers need not be in complete sentences. (2×½=1)

1) ....

2) ....

(e) Answer in a word or phrase each : (2 ×½=1)

1) How soon can an Eskimo build an igloo ?

....

2) What is the lamp and cooking pot made of ?

....